FINDING PARADISE IN SOUTH DAKOTA

GUN DOGS
PHEASANTS
PRAIRIE GROUSE
AND MORE

Endorsements

"Even though the author comes dangerously close to giving away some of my secret spots, I must admit this is one book all avid bird hunters will want on their shelf. I highly recommend it."
Jack Connelly, Principal Wildife Research Biologist, Idaho Department of Fish and Game, Blackfoot.

"One of the most entertaining hunting books you will find. Truly a great read for those enthusiasts that prefer the working man's approach." Dale Gates, Regional Conservation Officer Supervisor and Program Manager, Pierre, SD

"As another guy who told his wife we would stay (in SD) a couple of years but instead stayed for decades I can relate to this book. I seldom hunt but I found *Finding Paradise in South Dakota* interesting, informative, insightful, and introspective in regards to the author, the people, the geography, and the wildlife. A very enjoyable read whether you're familiar with South Dakota or not." Robert Dallman, Olathe, Kansas

"Terrific book, and I'm not even a hunter! I have never wanted to go to South Dakota...until now." Matt Pinnell, Springville, Utah

On Front cover: The cock pheasant in spring and male sharp-tailed grouse dancing on a lek are both courtesy of Bob Hodorff, Hot Springs, South Dakota. The Brittany (Brook) belongs to the author.

FINDING PARADISE IN SOUTH DAKOTA

GUN DOGS
PHEASANTS
PRAIRIE GROUSE
AND MORE

Lester D. Flake

LDFlake
PUBLISHING

Copyright © 2014 Lester D. Flake

This work may not be reproduced in any form without prior written permission from the author or his designates except in the case of brief passages embodied in critical reviews and articles.

ISBN-13: 978-1502979025
ISBN-10: 1502979020

Other books coauthored or senior authored by L.D. Flake

Willis, D.W., C.G. Scalet, and L.D. Flake. 2009. Introduction to wildlife and fisheries: An integrated approach. W.H. Freeman and Company, New York. 2nd edition.

Flake, L.D., C.P. Lehman, A.P. Leif, M.A. Rumble, and D.J. Thompson. 2006. The Wild Turkey in South Dakota. South Dakota Department of Game, Fish and Parks, Pierre, and South Dakota Agricultural Experiment Station, Brookings. SDAES B747.

Flake, L.D., J.W. Connelly, T.R. Kirschenmann, and A.J. Lindbloom. 2010. Grouse of Plains and Mountains—the South Dakota Story. South Dakota Department of Game, Fish and Parks, Pierre.

Flake, L.D., A. E. Gabbert, T.R. Kirschenmann, A.P. Leif, and C.T. Switzer. 2012. Ring-Necked Pheasants: Thriving in South Dakota. South Dakota Department of Game, Fish and Parks, Pierre.

Acknowledgements

Thanks to Gary Peterson, Jack Connelly, Mary Brashier, Gary Marrone, Dale Gates, Carter Johnson, Kurt Foreman, George Vandel, Matt Pinnell, and Bob Dallman for taking the interest to read extensive portions or all of the prepublication manuscript. I appreciate their encouragement and suggestions. I especially appreciate the many hours that Mary Brashier and Jack Connelly voluntarily put into reviewing and editing this book. Mary served many years as Agricultural Communications Editor at South Dakota State University and Jack has extensive experience in writing and editing for professional research journals as well as for popular magazines. Remaining errors in this book are strictly my own, probably made in late additions and post review edits.

Thanks to Doug Backlund (Wild Photos Photography, Pierre, SD) and Bob Hodorff (Hot Springs, SD) for the quality wildlife photos included herein. Bill Schultze was helpful in sending me photos from Sand Lake National Wildlife Refuge. Photographers for individual photos in the text (excluding my own) are acknowledged in captions. Thanks to my granddaughter, Sophia Shaw, for providing sketches. Gary Larson, South Dakota State University, helped me with plant names where I had questions.

Typesetting and formatting of the book for print was a new challenge for me and I was only successful because of guidance from Rachael Anderson. Rachael is a friend, neighbor, and author of several novels. Rachael also developed the attractive cover design.

I am especially appreciative for those South Dakota farmers and ranchers that continue to make efforts to retain grasslands, wetlands, and other cover needed by pheasants, sharp-tailed grouse, greater prairie-chickens, and a diversity of other wildlife species. I also express appreciation to the many South Dakota farmers and ranchers that so graciously give permission for responsible upland bird and waterfowl hunters to hunt on their land. I count several of these landowners among my best of friends.

To Marcia and our three children, Margo, Kim, and Ryan, for the many great South Dakota memories we share. Also, dedicated to all those that know and appreciate South Dakota's diverse wildlife species and the wetlands, native grasslands, and other habitats that provide places for these species to thrive.

Table of Contents

Part I. South Dakota—Careful, you will love it there 1
    Ch. 1. Moving to gun dog paradise..1
    Ch. 2. Exaggerated hunting reports and reality..5
    Ch. 3. Three is a crowd..7
    Ch. 4. A long season for pheasants and prairie grouse 10
    Ch. 5. Sleep late for pheasants, up early for prairie grouse 11

Part II. Thoughts on some places to hunt 13
    Ch. 6. Walk-in areas—just get out and start hunting 13
    Ch. 7. Game Production Areas and Waterfowl Production Areas 15
    Ch. 8. National Grasslands—lots of space and few hunters................................ 18
    Ch. 9. State School and Public Lands, meandered lakes 21
    Ch. 10. Other public areas... 23
    Ch. 11. Private lands—making good friends 25
    Ch. 12. Tribal lands.. 29
    Ch. 13. Fee access lands and commercial (licensed) pheasant preserves............ 30

Part III. Hunting the wily ringneck—challenges and tips 31
    Ch. 14. Roosters, roosters, and more roosters... 31
    Ch. 15. The Corn harvest—better than opening day 32
    Ch. 16. Wild and tricky ringnecks—run, run, run, runaway................................ 37
    Ch. 17. Outfoxing wily roosters... 39
    Ch. 18. Wide ranging pointing dogs and heavily hunted roosters 42
    Ch. 19. Late afternoon through sunset—the magic hours................................. 43
    Ch. 20. A freshly fallen snow 46
    Ch. 21. But someone just hunted that spot.. 49
    Ch. 22. Poor pheasant year—why show up?... 52
    Ch. 23. Lousy looking spots could be a surprise.. 54
    Ch. 24. Hunting over ice—and breaking through 58
    Ch. 25. Winter snows, cattails, and deer trails—gut check................................ 61
    Ch. 26. Pheasants—hanging close to food 65
    Ch. 27. Windy day birds 67
    Ch. 28. The coldest day.. 71
    Ch. 29. Hunting shelterbelts and childhood memories of an owl attack 74
    Ch. 30. A list of suggestions to improve your pheasant hunting success 77

Part IV. Prairie grouse—in the footsteps of pioneers 79
    Ch. 31. Two prairie grouse species... 79
    Ch. 32. Grouse hunting—getting started... 84
    Ch. 33. Fort Pierre National Grassland—memorable grouse hunts................... 86
    Ch. 34. Sorry, I've already promised the area to friends...................................... 92
    Ch. 35. You can hunt grouse but my ranch is pretty small.................................. 93
    Ch. 36. Badlands, sharptails, and rattlesnakes... 95
    Ch. 37. An Intermittent stream and grouse 97
    Ch. 38. Prairie grouse and Russian olives..100
    Ch. 39. Shrubs and more shrubs...102
    Ch. 40. Peering prairie grouse—it's about vegetation height............................103
    Ch. 41. Prairie grouse know it's warmer on the lee side.....................................105
    Ch. 42. A long trip home but time for one quick hunt.......................................107
    Ch. 43. A list of suggestions to improve your success hunting prairie grouse ..109

Part V. Gun dogs—keys to great hunts.. 112

Ch. 44. Getting started with your own hunting dog 112
Ch. 45. Training to retrieve 117
Ch. 46. Retrieving and misleading 119
Ch. 47. Bird dogs—warm, friendly, and mobile remote sensors 121
Ch. 48. Hey boss—pay attention 123
Ch. 49. Running with the dog 126
Ch. 50. Get back—it's a skunk! 127
Ch. 51. A bad guy kills my Brittany 130
Ch. 52. Gun dog and a pet mallard 132
Ch. 53. Gun dogs in the doghouse 135
Ch. 54. Walking my hunting dog—The amorous Pyrenees 137
Ch. 55. Pitbull attack on Thanksgiving 140
Ch. 56. Other interesting encounters for dogs 142
Ch. 57. Etiquette if you are invited to hunt over a bird dog 144

Part VI. Related memories and distractions 146
Ch. 58. Ducks and geese—lots of 'em 146
Ch. 59. High winds, ducks, and corn shucks 149
Ch. 60. Ice hole waterfowl, kids, and a pup 152
Ch. 61. Whitetails, pheasants, and more 156
Ch. 62. A campfire visit from a Charles Manson look-alike 159
Ch. 63. Camping with the mayor's permission 161
Ch. 64. Can pheasants swim? 162
Ch. 65. Holding tight! 164
Ch. 66. A nap to stay the distance 166
Ch. 67. Stocked pheasants—they needed wild mothers to teach them 168
Ch. 68. Distinguished guests and paradise 170
Ch. 69. Carter's hunting cabin—a few memories 176
Ch. 70. More hunting cabin memories, loss of a good friend 180
Ch. 71. Meandered lakes and changing habitats 183
Ch. 72. Hunting and staying out of trouble at home 185
Ch. 73. Loose feathers, spurs, and processed game birds 188
Ch. 74. These birds didn't come out of a grocery store 191
Ch. 75. Don't overcook game birds 192
Ch. 76. As a nonresident—tripping to paradise and back 194
Ch. 77. Neophyte hunters—a bit scary 196
Ch. 78. Chinook salmon and prairie grouse 198

Part VII. Threats to the South Dakota paradise 201
Ch. 79. Wetlands, wildlife, and sinking duck boats 201
Ch. 80. More row crops and less cover mean fewer pheasants 207
Ch. 81. Disappearing native grasslands, prairie grouse, and memories 210
Ch. 82. Still a paradise for bird hunting 213
Ch. 83 Epilogue 217

Partial glossary of terms 219
About the author 224
Additional related photos 225
MAP 232

Foreword

When bird hunters talk of pheasant hunting experiences or even of plans or dreams of the future, South Dakota is often mentioned as a premiere destination. In this book, I somewhat emphasize ring-necked pheasants because they are the primary upland game bird that most hunters associate with South Dakota. Still, sharp-tailed grouse and greater prairie-chickens are both exciting birds to hunt. Furthermore, they are most often associated with beautiful native prairies and the diversity of life these prairies support. For grouse enthusiasts, sharp-tailed grouse (sharptails) and prairie chickens provide a hunting experience for native game that can't be matched by pheasants.

Hunters that learn I lived in South Dakota for 31 years and have hunted upland game there for 41 years, often express their desire to hunt in that state and ask for suggestions on hunting. Even people with little hunting experience and without a trained gundog commonly express their interest and dreams of someday hunting ring-necked pheasants in South Dakota. This book is especially written for upland game hunters that have a hunting dog, intend to get a hunting dog, or that hunt with a good friend that owns a hunting dog. It is also written for those who plan to hunt alone or in very small groups. Nonresident upland game hunters who are unfamiliar with South Dakota will especially benefit from reading this book and considering approaches that will help make their hunt successful. Residents who have not hunted pheasants or prairie grouse or who have minimal experience hunting upland birds will also benefit. Those who are already veteran pheasant hunters will enjoy and directly relate to many of the stories and experiences. Readers that do not hunt or seldom hunt will enjoy some of the crazy stories.

I was fortunate that my profession took me to South Dakota State University (SDSU) in Brookings in 1972 where I had accepted a faculty position in the Department of Wildlife and Fisheries Sciences (now the Department of Natural Resource Management). It was a great place to live, for our three children to grow up, and for a rewarding teaching and research career. On retirement from SDSU in 2003, my wife Marcia and I moved to Utah to be closer to my wife's aging mother and to our children and their families in California and Utah. Since that time I have not given up my interest in South Dakota, in the state's marvelous upland game hunting, or in seeing my many friends in that state. In fact, I have returned each year in the fall to hunt pheasants, prairie grouse (sharp-tailed grouse and greater prairie-chickens), and sometimes ducks; to work on a series of wildlife books for the Department of Game, Fish and Parks (completed); and to visit friends. I still know people all over the state.

For me, the thrill of watching a gun dog work is an essential part of upland bird hunting. My hunting companions and I usually hunt on public land; private land leased for hunting access by the South Dakota Department of Game, Fish and Parks (SDGFP); or on private land by permission. I have a few long-time friends that have farms with excellent wildlife habitat but those friendships often started when I asked for permission to hunt. If you are willing to get out of the vehicle and work for birds you will have no problem finding sufficient public access (public lands or leased walk-in areas) to keep you occupied. There are still many landowners who will allow single hunters or small groups (like two or three hunters) access for hunting if permission is requested, especially if it is not the opening day or week of the general season. Even if you are turned down, you will find most South Dakota landowners are nice folks.

I purposely give only the first name of most landowners mentioned in connection with hunting spots so as not to send extra traffic in that direction. I also have been rather general about favorite hunting spots. A few hunting friends have promised to "get even" if I revealed any of their favorite haunts.

Part I. South Dakota—Careful, you will love it there

Ch. 1. Moving to gun dog paradise

In 1970 I had taken a temporary instructor position in the Biology Department at Fresno State University while still completing my dissertation in Zoology and Physiology at Washington State University. I had interviewed at Fresno State shortly after radicals had bombed and destroyed the main frame computer room. Fortunately, things tamed down at Fresno State after that incident. The temporary position at Fresno State lasted just two years but gave me some important teaching experience. Even with teaching experience, it was tough to compete for the limited college faculty positions in Zoology, Biology, or related areas.

In August of 1972, I received a call from the Department Head of Wildlife and Fisheries Sciences, Dr. John Gates, at South Dakota State University (SDSU), just a month after ending my temporary contract at Fresno State. A few weeks later, John Gates picked me up at the Sioux Falls Airport for my interview and we drove the 50 miles north on Interstate 29 to Brookings through a glacial landscape of farms, cropland, pastures, wetlands, and shelterbelts. As we exited the off ramp to Brookings, a hen pheasant flew just in front of the vehicle and landed in the grass-forb cover between the off ramp and the freeway. That pheasant was a glimpse of what was to come, a vision into the many years I would live in South Dakota.

The interview and my lecture to students and faculty in the Department of Wildlife and Fisheries Sciences went well and I was soon offered a teaching and research position in the Department. This move would mean being a long way from family members on the west coast and from Marcia's parents in Idaho (and later Utah). Marcia knew I needed a good professional start and we accepted the job in South Dakota. I promised Marcia we would stay only a couple of years and then find a position closer to family in the west. I even felt a little guilty about accepting the position while knowing all along that Marcia was depending on me moving back west soon. Now I suspect the folks that hired me knew I would love South Dakota and SDSU and that we would likely stay a long time.

I was too busy getting lectures ready to hunt more than a few days that first fall plus I had to get 10-day nonresident licenses until I qualified for residency. However, a couple of late season hunts over Don and Shirley Ann Hales enthusiastic Brittany got me to thinking about gun dogs and pheasants and hoping I could convince Marcia we needed to get a Brittany for a family pet and stay a few years longer. Don was a fellow faculty member in my Department plus we shared activity in the same small church. We still keep in touch. And yes, I did get my first Brittany the very next spring (1973).

It was a late November day in the mid-1970s and it had snowed about six inches two days earlier. I had permission to hunt on private land about 15 miles west of Brookings and I headed directly for a four-acre wetland dominated by cattails and bulrush in all but the open center. Three weeks earlier the center of that wetland had provided some dynamite evening duck hunting but it was now covered with about four inches of ice. Numerous pheasant tracks marked the snow along the wetland's edge and my Brittany, Pepsi, followed fresh scent into cattail cover. She was soon locked on point and a colorful, long-tailed rooster burst into flight, cackling in the bright fall sun, in easy reach of my 12 gauge pump. It was a calm day with temperatures around freezing—a day when pheasant hunting was unbelievably perfect. Pepsi retrieved the bird and I admired the colorful feathers and long tail—there would be more points on roosters before the day ended.

How could I move back to California, Oregon, Washington or other places closer to family as I had promised Marcia when we had moved here a few years ago. This was paradise! People warned me that South Dakota could be extremely cold in late fall and winter but I never seemed to notice until pheasant season ended. And even then, I usually forgot the cold in the midst of family life, work at the University, ice fishing, and so many other activities. Also, the reputation for constant winter cold in eastern

South Dakota seems a bit exaggerated to me. Fortunately, or perhaps unfortunately for my wife Marcia, I had fallen in love with South Dakota. Eventually, in many ways, she would too.

Let me warn you! If you are an upland game hunter be careful about going to South Dakota, don't move there, don't make friends there, and especially, don't hunt there—it is too much fun, too addicting, too hard to leave. You will always want just one last hunt, one last chance to work your hunting dog, one last bird at close range. Of course I am being facetious about staying away from South Dakota. South Dakota can truly be a wonderland for upland game hunters. I know, I have hunted South Dakota for 41 years and loved every minute.

With such a great job, terrific people, excellent schools, and the best all-around bird hunting in North America it was difficult to consider leaving for another faculty position or other job. Soon our growing family was deeply tied to South Dakota and our three children, Margo, Kim, and Ryan, did not want to leave their friends and schools. Marcia's teaching position at Brookings High School gave her more reasons for staying. The two years turned into 31 years from September of 1972 until August of 2003 before I retired and honored my promise to take Marcia back west so she could help her aging mother in Utah.

Since moving to Springville, Utah, in August 2003, I have returned to South Dakota each fall to hunt pheasants and grouse, visit friends, take photos, and work on wildlife books . Leaving South Dakota after retirement was the most difficult move I have ever made. The people, open spaces, wildlife, glacial wetlands, and native prairies were some of the things I most loved. And of course, so much great bird hunting!

I promised Marcia (photo from early 1980s) we would only stay in South Dakota a couple of years. I sure broke that promise! She is holding our second Brittany, Rascal.

Muskrat houses on a glacial marsh in eastern South Dakota. One of the many reasons I loved living there.

Ch. 2. Exaggerated hunting reports and reality

Reports of almost unbelievable pheasant abundance in South Dakota in the mid-1930s and 1940s (World War II) when much agricultural land was left idle and grown up in weedy cover are mostly true. Indeed, pheasant abundance during some of these periods was spectacular. Peaks in pheasant abundance from the late 1950s to the mid-1960s during the Soil Bank Era and in the 1990s and early 2000s (Conservation Reserve Program) when much agricultural land was retired in protective grass and forb cover have also been impressive. Still, in the 41 years I have hunted South Dakota's private and public land for pheasants I have rarely bagged my limit in an hour or less of total hunting time during the day. Oh, to be sure, it does happen sometimes but not often. In those cases I actually felt a little disappointed because I wanted to hunt longer. Even when I see hundreds of birds in one day, they are usually wild and wary with many flushing far ahead of the gun. I do have friends that own or have access to private lands managed just for great pheasant hunting and they sometimes report seeing incredible numbers of pheasants and taking limits easily. Such hunts are the exception, even in South Dakota. Many nonresidents wanting to hunt South Dakota have an overblown vision of bird abundance and ease of the hunt.

A typical hunt with your gun dog in South Dakota will involve plenty of work for the cock pheasants (or prairie grouse) that flush in good shooting range. As a resident most of my pheasant hunting, except on Saturday, occurred late in the afternoon for a couple of hours. I almost always have success or chances at success even when only hunting late in the day. When I have hunted full days (hours for pheasants are 12:00 Central the first week and 10:00 Central thereafter; see regulations), I do not kill limits every day even when hunting hard and long. In my favorite hunting areas my best days might involve limiting on pheasants and prairie grouse (sharp-tailed grouse and greater prairie-chickens). In some cases, especially in the northern part of the state, a few coveys of gray partridge might also be flushed during the day. With this said, I also have plenty of memories of hunting all day, muffing some opportunities, and ending up skunked.

During my 31 years as a South Dakota resident, I always hunted hard while I was in the field. I think it was an inherited characteristic. I could never seem to slow down. Today, as a nonresident, I am even more determined to make good use of my time in South Dakota by getting into the field, walking miles of cover, and burning those calories every day regardless of the weather. I appreciate every day my knees hold up and I train hard in the off season so I can keep moving, pushing the cover, and hunting upland game. Wild birds, tough hunts, exciting hunts, and gun dogs—that is the South Dakota experience.

Like this giant pheasant on the east side of Huron, reports on South Dakota pheasant hunting often get a bit exaggerated.

Ch. 3. Three is a crowd

My greatest nightmare for hunting pheasants is walking a large standing corn or grain sorghum field with other "walkers" and with "blockers" at the end of the rows. This popular pheasant hunting strategy is a good way to get pheasants but could also be the quickest way to get shot. On a November day in the 1980s a friend told me that they really needed me to help walk a cornfield that was loaded with hundreds of pheasants. Blockers were placed at one end and about six of us spread out and started walking through the field. To make it worse, at least half of the other hunters were complete strangers to me. The walkers were quickly a little out of line, pheasants started jumping, and multiple shots were fired. This all made me plenty nervous plus controlling my Brittany in a standing cornfield was tough if not impossible. I pulled my dog in and had her walk at "heel." Then I walked forward with my head and eyes towards the ground (for protection) and with trepidation that I might be hit in an eye with errant shot. I did not attempt to shoot and solidly vowed to stay out of "walking and blocking" situations with groups of hunters. I have done so! The danger of being hit by stray pellets on this type of hunt is evident in the annual report of hunting injuries in the South Dakota Conservation Digest. Be sure you wear safety glasses if you go on a "walking and blocking" pheasant hunt.

This book is mostly for upland bird hunters that like to hunt alone or with a friend or two using a gun dog or dogs. A person without a hunting dog could also use many of the hunting approaches included herein. If you hunt without a gun dog I suggest you walk slowly like you would in "still" hunting white-tailed deer since that seems to allow you to get close to birds and to make them flush, probably because the pheasants get nervous. Then make sure you try to take only close, killing shots since pheasants so often run after being shot and, without a good dog, your crippling rates are likely to increase greatly. Snow cover, especially fresh snow, also helps if you are hunting without a gun dog since you can so easily locate bird concentrations from the pheasant tracks.

Sometimes I am told that seniors my age should not hunt alone but I ignore that instruction if it is not convenient for a friend to go with me. For safety in case of an accident or medical problems I carry a cell phone and a "finder" GPS unit that can send out a rescue signal. In my opinion, hunting pheasants alone is not nearly as risky as hunting in larger groups. And, it is much more effective and fun.

My favorite way of hunting is with a long-time hunting friend with both of us having a hunting dog. I have hunted this way with a few long-time acquaintances and I value their friendship and especially like to hunt with them. With my hunting friends, we only shoot our own birds and never go for a group limit as sometimes practiced with larger groups. There is no one I have hunted with more than Dale Gates of Pierre. Dale and I both run Brittanys and we usually hunt on larger areas where we both know where the other person is but where the dogs do not interfere with each other. We both know about what the other person will do in most hunting situations. Dale's wife Natalie told us "you guys don't really hunt together at all, you both take off in separate directions." Okay, Natalie is correct. We are often from 200 yards to a quarter mile or more apart but periodically verify that the other person is alive and okay. Sight contact is usually sufficient. When we grouse hunt together on the open grasslands such as on Fort Pierre National Grassland, we are often even much farther apart. I like that kind of hunting!

Dale Gates is a Regional Conservation Officer Supervisor and Program Manager in the Pierre region for the South Dakota Department of Game, Fish and Parks (SDGFP). Natalie is also a wildlife biologist but is with the U.S. Fish and Wildlife Service in Pierre. I have known Dale since he was in grade school when he accompanied me on hunting trips even before he carried a gun. Dale's father, John Gates, was the Department Head of the Wildlife and Fisheries Sciences Department at South Dakota State University that I had first met when he picked me up at the airport for my interview for a faculty position in September of 1972. Dr. Gates was a great person and a much accomplished research biologist, teacher, and administrator. Sadly, John Gates died of cancer in his early 40s, just about a year after we moved to South Dakota. I have remained friends with his wife Connie, Dale, and Dale's older brother Bob, now a wildlife research biologist and professor at Ohio State University. Connie still keeps her own Brittany and often takes care of my Brittany for me during non-hunting hours when I am in Brookings. You can accurately call her home the "Brittany palace" (see related photo at end of book) because Brittanys live like royalty in that house under her kindly hand.

Natalie, Dale's wife, was my graduate student at South Dakota State University. I told Natalie that Dale was a pretty neat guy but she told me she thought he was already spoken for by another young lady. I replied that I didn't think so. They ended up getting married and now I stay at their home for several days each fall while Dale and I pursue pheasants and prairie grouse.

Dale Gates and his two French Brittanys, Eddy (left) and BJ, after hunting a public access area near Pierre in 2013. I have hunted with Dale since before he carried a gun.

Ch. 4. A long season for pheasants and prairie grouse

South Dakota's general pheasant season starts the third Saturday in October and for the last several years has extended into the first week-end in January, almost 3 months of great hunting. While pheasant populations can easily stand the long hunting seasons, political pressure during years when pheasant numbers are relatively low have sometimes forced earlier closures. Pheasant hunting is good through the entire season, especially if you get moderate amounts of snow later in the year to concentrate the birds and help hold them in heavy cover.

The hunting season for sharp-tailed grouse, greater prairie-chickens, and gray partridge is a month longer than the pheasant season, opening the third Saturday in September and running until the end of pheasant season in early January. Prairie grouse (meaning sharp-tailed grouse and greater prairie-chickens herein) in my experience have provided excellent hunting over a gun dog through mid-November but get extremely wild and difficult to approach by mid to late season. Dale Gates of Pierre told me he has had success taking greater prairie-chickens and sharp-tailed grouse over his pointing dog in early January during mild winters with little or no snow accumulation. Although the flocks sometimes held for points, he noted that grouse broke from cover farther out in these late hunts and that you needed to be quick to get up to your gun dog and to get off an effective shot. If there is a lot of snow on the ground the grouse usually see you coming from a distance and will flush far out of range. However, if they are using juniper, Russian olive, silver buffaloberry, wild plum or other woodland or tall shrub areas during late season, as sharptails sometimes do, approach during snowy years may be more feasible. Generally, for the best prairie grouse hunting I recommend hunting earlier in the season.

Ch. 5. Sleep late for pheasants, up early for prairie grouse

Pheasant hunters in South Dakota should be aware of the rather odd shooting hours. During opening week hunting starts at noon in the Central Time Zone. After the first week the shooting time changes to 10 a.m. Central Time. In the Mountain Time zone (most of West River South Dakota), the opener starts at 11 a.m. and, after the first week, hunters can begin pheasant hunting at 9 a.m. Grouse and gray partridge open at sunrise and all upland birds close at sunset. Be sure to check the South Dakota *Hunting and Trapping Handbook* published each year to confirm season dates and shooting hours.

My friends and I often hunt areas in central or northern South Dakota that have mixed species of upland birds but we commonly hold off hunting until around the opening hour for pheasants since the day can get rather long. Also, hunting for grouse and partridge early in the morning invariably involves some close up points or flushes on cock pheasants before legal shooting hours for pheasants—a frustrating situation for both dog and hunter. We often use that morning time to enjoy a leisurely breakfast and to get to know some of the local residents. In the smallest towns, there is often only one café and the morning gatherings and conversations can be a clearly valuable asset to the social fabric and health of the community. My friends and I have great memories of some of these daily gatherings and of old timers that joined our table.

In the early 1990s I stumbled into a perfect in-class demonstration of law enforcement and the noon opening hours during the first week of pheasant season. I had taken our senior wildlife management class on a field trip near Whitewood Lake west of Brookings with two South Dakota Game, Fish and Parks (SDGFP) professionals, Dan Limmer and Shane Van Bockern. It was the first week of pheasant season. Dan and Shane were talking to about 15 of our senior students regarding their work with SDGFP, part of which involved law enforcement. We were standing at a gravel road intersection on a hill a few miles east of Lake Whitewood with section line roads sloping off in four directions. The spot provided a nice landscape view for talking about wildlife habitat. As we were visiting, a vehicle about a half mile to the south stopped, two guys jumped out, and blazed away with their shotguns. It was about 11 a.m. and well before pheasant shooting was legal. Dan and Shane jumped in a vehicle, quickly drove to the scene of the violation, and apprehended the two surprised men who were retrieving the illegally taken pheasant. That arrest made for an interesting experience for each of the students to observe; some of those same students soon became conservation officers. No, it was not staged.

A hen pheasant flew across the freeway off ramp as we turned into Brookings for my job interview in 1972. Looking back, that sure seems appropriate. (Courtesy of Bob Hodorff)

Part II. Thoughts on some places to hunt

Ch. 6. Walk-in areas—just get out and start hunting

Fortunately, the South Dakota Department of Game, Fish and Parks (SDGFP) contracts with many landowners to allow foot traffic for hunting purposes. These walk-in areas, Conservation Reserve Enhancement Program (CREP) lands, and other private lands leased for public hunting access are clearly mapped in each year's *South Dakota Hunting Atlas*; they are also marked with signs in the field. Copies of the Atlas are available at most stores that sell hunting equipment and in SDGFP regional offices. They can also be ordered in late summer or fall over the Internet from the SDGFP. Maps can be downloaded on your GPS so you can know exactly where you are on the walk-in or other leased areas.

For simplicity, I generally refer to all of these lands leased for hunting by the SDGFP as walk-in areas. Private lands leased for hunting by the SDGFP are the primary areas I hunt for pheasants and prairie grouse in the central and West River areas of the state. Those in the western prairie regions lacking intermixed cropland may have few or no pheasants but provide for expansive areas with good prairie grouse hunting. Of course, opening day of pheasant season can be crowded on the better areas open to public access but the season is long, and after the opening week or two, these areas receive much less pressure. In many cases you can clearly tell if walk-in areas are suitable for pheasants, prairie grouse, or both but in other situations you will need to hunt the areas to determine the upland bird composition. Those exploratory hunts can be fun and you will undoubtedly discover some great spots while getting plenty of exercise and, usually, some shooting.

Finding Paradise in South Dakota

As a heads up, some of the CREP lands established in the James River Valley in places like Marshall and Brown counties are turning out to be hot spots for some of the best hunting in the state. Even in 2013, a year with predicted low numbers of pheasants, CREP areas provided some phenomenal mid and late season hunting for pheasants.

Both pheasants and sharp-tailed grouse made for a great hunt on this West River walk-in area.

Ch. 7. Game Production Areas and Waterfowl Production Areas

It was early November and I had traveled about an hour west of Brookings with the intention of hunting pheasants on some public areas I had not hunted before. There were several state owned Game Production Areas (GPAs) and federally owned Waterfowl Production Areas (WPAs) within an 8 mile radius of the glacial hill where I was parked, all color marked in the *South Dakota Hunting Atlas*. Both WPAs and GPAs are purchased and the taxes paid for primarily by sportsmen's dollars. Most of these funds come from hunter license fees, a federal tax on arms and ammunition (Pittman Robertson Act or Federal Aid in Wildlife Restoration Act), and from Migratory Bird Hunting and Conservation Stamps (WPAs). Every time I see one of these areas, I am thankful for the folks at both federal and state levels that thought ahead to try and set aside some habitat for wildlife.

As hunters, we should have positive feelings knowing we are able to help out with funding these special places. Hunters are paying most of the costs of purchase, taxes, and other expenses involved in keeping this habitat for wildlife. Many of the wetlands on these areas would have been drained long ago without such programs; the grassland cover tilled under; the habitat left wanting; and many wildlife species hurting for places to nest, rest, winter, and otherwise live. Plus, we would not have such easily and freely available access to tens of thousands of acres of hunting lands.

I parked my vehicle at a public area I had never hunted that was a combination of GPA and WPA lands. It covered over 1,300 acres with a large wetland in the center. The habitat looked good and included extensive areas of intermediate and tall wheatgrass along with some uplands seeded into native tallgrasses like switchgrass, Indiangrass, and big bluestem. I was encouraged to see dense stands of emergent plants (cattail, bulrushes, etc.) around the periphery of the large wetland and in some other smaller wetlands on the site. I knew that the dense drawdown and emergent vegetation growing in moist soils and shallow water areas would help hold some of the pheasants that my dog and I would likely push ahead of us from the uplands. I noted recently harvested cornfields that bordered the public area—plenty of waste grain for pheasants. I was confident the area had good numbers of pheasants and I could see only one other vehicle parked over a mile away on the opposite side from where I was parked. I was not surprised at the lack of pressure since competition on public areas is usually low after the first couple of weeks of hunting.

The hunt turned out to be a productive one, the pheasants wild and challenging, the terrain and vegetation a test of physical condition. Two of the three roosters I shot that day were pushed from the upland grasses by my Brittany and trailed into cattail patches on the edge of the large wetland. In thick patches of cattail they held tight for close-up points. I will never get over the thrill and sound of roosters flushing out of dense cattails at close, mind rattling range. Neither will you!

Even on the opening Saturday of the general pheasant season hunters can find GPAs and WPAs with plenty of space to safely hunt and work their gun dogs and with adequate numbers of pheasants (and in some areas prairie grouse) to keep the hunt interesting. Parts of the state with comparatively lower pheasant brood counts often have good hunting and will have much less competition than more popular public hunting areas during the opening week of the pheasant season.

Game Production Areas and Waterfowl Production Areas are especially abundant in eastern South Dakota on highland areas (Missouri Coteau and Prairie Coteau) with rockier glacial soils and abundant wetlands. If you are hunting nothing but these two types of public areas, you will usually have a rewarding hunt in South Dakota as long as you have a gun dog with a good nose. And, if you hunt during mid to late season you will generally find little competition.

Finding Paradise in South Dakota

Waterfowl Production Areas (WPAs)
benefit a wide variety of wildlife species and provide great
hunting opportunities.

Reynold's Slough Game Production Area (GPA) features a
beautiful mixture of upland and wetland cover.

Ch. 8. National Grasslands—lots of space and few hunters

The rolling grasslands on Fort Pierre National Grassland (FPNG)(116,000 acres) extended before us for miles with patches of interspersed private cropland showing here and there. It was late October and Dale Gates and I were working our two Brittanys and staying within occasional sight of each other. The prairie birds, plants, and terrain blended together, providing an amazingly beautiful fall setting. The overall experience of hunting on the native prairie was exhilarating! Temperatures would reach close to 65 degrees Fahrenheit with minimal winds on that day—what a great day to be afield. We were flushing pheasants in the heavier cover spots, especially near private cropland, but mostly greater prairie-chickens and lesser numbers of sharp-tailed grouse in the lighter mixed grass cover. We were having good success and we had seen only one other hunter all morning. This is what you might expect when hunting on the FPNG if you take the time to get to know the habitat on these lands and if you hunt after the opening weekend of the grouse season (third Saturday in September). Even opening weekend is not really very crowded if you are willing to walk.

Production of young grouse and pheasants is far greater on FPNG in more moist years than during severe drought. Bird production is also greatly influenced by pasture management decisions made out of the FPNG office in Pierre. Nesting birds fare much better during periods when staff at the FPNG has strong leadership interested in improving the grasslands for wildlife as well as managing for improved pastures for cattle. Without responsible and enlightened Forest Service leadership on National Grasslands, some grazing lessees have a tendency to allow their their cattle to reduce coverage of grasses and forbs to the detriment of grouse, other wildlife, and, eventually, even cattle.

If you hunt the Grande River National Grassland (GRNG)(155,000 acres) in northwestern South Dakota during more moist years with good grass-forb cover, you can find pheasants and gray partridge in some of the areas closer to cropland. However, most of the extensive grassland is sharp-tailed grouse habitat so pheasants and partridge are usually secondary species on the hunt. During a series of moist years, this vast national grassland can provide rewarding hunting for upland game birds with almost no competition from other hunters. Time and experience hunting the grassland and reading the cover will improve your success. For example, if you find spots with lots of legumes and other forbs mixed with the grasses you will normally find better hunting for sharp-tailed grouse. Pheasants are also attracted to legumes and other mixed forbs, especially if the cover is relatively tall and dense for the GRNG. One day I saw a flock of about 30 wild turkeys near a woody bottomland on GRNG, so you might want to look into fall turkey permits as well.

The Buffalo Gap National Grassland (BGNG) (600,000 acres) supports pheasants in some areas with adequate cover near private cropland but most of the area is primarily sharp-tailed grouse habitat. Buffalo Gap has the driest climate of the three national grasslands in South Dakota. During a series of moist years, BGNG can be good hunting for sharptails. Much of the Buffalo Gap National Grassland can look particularly sparse in terms of good cover during drought years due to cattle grazing and lack of plant growth. In drought years cattle generally remove much of the limited plant growth and bird production and bird hunting are usually poor.

The boundaries of the national grasslands are clearly marked in the *South Dakota Hunting Atlas*. Hunters can expect the national grasslands to have lots of space and minimal competition. Observant hunters can learn to read the habitat on these areas and have some good, even great, uncrowded bird hunting. I love to hunt each of the national grasslands in South Dakota but I know it can take time to figure out how to find the better hunting pastures. For hunters that enjoy hiking and running their gun dog while checking the huge pastures on the national grasslands, I would say give it a try.

A few words of caution on the national grasslands. Keep your dog away from black-tailed prairie dog towns because of the concentration of prairie rattlesnakes on these areas. The loud "chirping" of the prairie dogs will usually let you know you are getting too close to a dog town. Another recommendation, if a pasture looks like it has been grazed heavily, do not bother to get out of the vehicle. In some pastures you could run into problems with prickly pear cactus in densities thick enough to cause problems for your dog. It pays to have pliers on hand.

The national grassland areas can be a puzzle for bird hunters. If you learn how to put the pieces together you will find a treasure in terms of upland bird hunting in an uncrowded environment.

National grasslands cover hundreds of thousands of acres in South Dakota and generally have few upland bird hunters. Buffalo Gap National Grassland near Ward Dam shown here. (Photo courtesy of Bob Hodorff)

Ch. 9. State School and Public Lands, meandered lakes

South Dakota's extensive State School and Public Lands are open to hunting as long as you avoid driving on the areas (unless a road is specifically marked as open) and as long as you avoid unharvested crops. These state lands are extensive and are color marked on the *South Dakota Hunting Atlas*. If you find an area of State School and Public Lands with grass and forb cover of sufficient height and density for pheasants and grouse to reproduce and find hiding cover, you might try hunting the area. If it is near cropland the area will normally have pheasants and if it is in a region where grassland covers more than 50% of the landscape it could also be good for prairie grouse. Again, you need to explore to find those great spots that will bring you back again and again. If a tract of school land is heavily grazed, as is the case for some, I would look farther for better grass and forb cover.

Meandered lakes are usually known by state residents but are not well advertised. These lakes and large wetlands were unsurveyed sites when the state was originally surveyed and they are basically recognized as public areas. Information on these lakes is available at the Register of Deeds Office in Pierre. Meandered lakes are usually known by the locals but the legalities of shoreline access (normal high water lines often not defined) are sometimes unclear so I will just tell you that many such lakes or wetlands exist in East River South Dakota and that they can harbor numerous pheasants in the dense shoreline cover or in the dry lakebeds (during drier periods). Such areas also often have good waterfowl hunting. Over the past 41 years, I have watched meandered lakes such as Lake Thompson and Lake Preston in Kingsbury County slowly change from dry or nearly dry lakebeds in the drier years to fishing lakes with walleye (Lake Thompson), yellow perch, and other game fish in the years after 1985. Many early settlers knew of such large-scale succession from shallow marshes to fishing lakes and from fishing lakes to nearly dry marshes since they had seen such changes occur through the decades.

The pattern of succession from emergent wetlands to lakes (and back again) is a natural cycle but the lake phase is probably increasing in frequency due to the unfortunate drainage of so many smaller wetlands in the respective drainage basins. The water once held by the smaller wetlands, instead of staying in place and helping conserve water on a local basis, floods downstream into the larger meandered lakes or down river systems. This is one of the reasons for the serious flooding problems we have seen so often in recent years in the upper Midwest. Seems irrational that with the surpluses in crop production of corn and some other crops, that we are still draining these valuable wetlands to get more crop production.

Lake Thompson is probably the largest meandered lake in South Dakota. It has gone through incredible changes from a shallow marsh during much of the past century to an extensive fishing lake during the past 25 years. Lake Thompson was still a dry or shallow marsh for the first approximately 13 years (1972-1985) I lived in South Dakota. The wetland basin was over seven miles long and four miles wide. The entire wetland was mostly moist wetland soil with extensive stands of cattails, phragmites (common reed grass), various bulrushes, and other wetland plants. Pheasants and white-tailed deer used the area extensively and concentrated in the protective cover in the winters. I often hunted the cover around the edges of this dry marsh near adjacent private cropland and waste grain where the pheasants were most abundant.

If you have the time and energy to look into these potential hunting areas, meandered lakes can provide some great pheasant hunting especially in the drier years. Later in the book, I share a little about hunting the shoreline of a meandered lake in the chapters titled "Carter's hunting cabin—a few memories" and "Meandered lakes and changing habitats."

Ch. 10. Other public areas

Sand Lake National Wildlife Refuge (Sand Lake NWR) in northeastern South Dakota and Lacreek National Wildlife Refuge in southwestern South Dakota can provide good pheasant hunting. Sand Lake (NWR) provides extensive areas to hunt and is often loaded with pheasants. However, it does not open up for pheasants until early December. The refuge covers 21,498 acres of upland and wetland habitats. Most of the area is open to pheasant hunting. There are normally very few hunters afield and, as noted in the chapter on "The Coldest Hunt," temperatures can be frigid. Still, I have hunted Sand Lake NWR in a lightweight hunting shirt, with temperatures in the mid 50s during a snowless December. Look at the weather forecast before making the trip to Sand Lake—try to avoid an approaching arctic clipper. Sand Lake NWR is a major stopover for migrating snow geese but these geese will have left the area by time the December pheasant hunt opens.

Sand Lake National Wildlife Refuge in December (Courtesy of Don Soderlund).

Lacreek National Wildlife Refuge (Lacreek NWR) has good pheasant as well as moderate to good sharp-tailed grouse populations and is located in southwestern South Dakota, an area with considerably warmer late fall and winter temperatures than Sand Lake NWR. Portions of the 16,410-acre refuge are closed to pheasant and grouse hunting so be sure to look for areas marked as open for hunting. The season dates are usually the same as for outside the refuge. The habitat includes upland grass-forb cover; wetland cover such as dense cattails, river bulrush, phragmites, and sandbar willow clumps; and nearby cropland for food (mostly on private land). While hunting you will also enjoy watching the many flocks of Canada geese, sandhill cranes, and ducks moving about the area. Lacreek NWR as well as nearby walk-in areas and Game Production areas can draw crowds for the opener and also seem to have more than the normal number of hunters (for South Dakota) even later in the season. For that reason, I tend to hunt less well-known areas.

Corps of Engineers land primarily along portions of the Missouri River and Bureau of Reclamation lands around Shadehill Reservoir provide opportunities for pheasant and grouse hunting if you are willing to walk and explore. Some of the less well-known areas that require hunters to walk a moderate distance can have surprisingly good hunting with little chance of seeing other hunters. If you take the time to hunt Corp of Engineers or Bureau of Reclamation areas you will likely find your own "little known" hot spots for pheasants as well as prairie grouse. Scattered Bureau of Land Management grasslands in western South Dakota can likewise provide uncrowded areas productive for sharp-tailed grouse.

Ch. 11. Private lands—making good friends

It was a clear early November day in the late 1970s and my father-in-law Ruel Allen and I were pursuing pheasants on a large Waterfowl Production Area (WPA) about 25 miles from Brookings. We were working plenty hard to get birds and had taken a couple of roosters. Bordering the WPA to the west was a square mile of private land, beautiful land, with several wetlands, lowland draws with good cover, and intermixed croplands. My Brittany Pepsi pushed beyond the fence line onto the private land, wanting to follow pheasants into some great cover but we did not have permission. I called Pepsi back. I remember wishing I had permission to hunt the private land and deciding I needed to get up the courage to find the landowner and ask. I don't know why there is always a little fear of asking since most farmers or landowners I have talked to have been really nice, even if for various reasons they do not allow you to hunt. Sometimes, they just want to reserve the area for part of the season for family.

As we approached the farmhouse, the landowner came to the door and we both recognized each other from when he and a friend had picked up a Brittany puppy from me a few years earlier in the mid 1970s. Bill had recently moved to this farm and taken over management of this family land from his father. I didn't know that he was not letting people hunt on his land so I asked if my father-in-law and I could hunt pheasants. I think Bill was even surprised when he said yes, we could hunt. It has been over 30 years and four hunting dogs since then and I'm still hunting on this farm and always visiting this family when I get to South Dakota. I've even gotten to know their farm dogs over the years and I know all the best hunting places on the farm. Some of the stories in this book, such as "Get back—it's a skunk," are from this farm.

Another time, I was headed out to hunt pheasants with Ruel a few miles southwest of Brookings in a wide grass and cattail drainage with crops on either side of the drainage. I knew Cal was almost always home so I was confident I could find him to get permission. A half mile from his home, a couple of roosters flew across the road into cover on his place. We found Cal at the farmhouse and I told him I had just watched those roosters fly in and asked if we could hunt. Cal's answer was much to the affirmative and to the point. "You don't ever need to ask me!" "Get out there and get those roosters right now!" Cal was a bachelor and I counted him as a friend from when I first met him in the 1970s until his death almost 30 years later—a kind and gentle soul, and such a good person. That's how it can be when you get to know farmers and ranchers in South Dakota.

Be sure to remember that hunting on private land without permission can result in loss of your hunting privileges for the year. When you ask for permission to hunt on private land there are some things to keep in mind. The more people with you the less chance landowners will let you hunt. To me, that seems only a natural reaction and I would feel the same if it were my farm. I have almost always been alone or with no more than two other people when I have sought permission to hunt on private land. Do not bring a crowd—ever!

Even on farms or ranches where I know the family well, I am reluctant to ever take more than two people with me in a hunting group and it is rare for me to take that many. Jack Connelly and Doug Finicle, both from Idaho, and I were eating supper at a bar in a small West River town with great pheasant and grouse hunting in the area (during some years) and with a number of nearby walk-in areas available for hunting. Jack is a grouse biologist with the Idaho Department of Fish and Wildlife and Doug is an engineer farmer in southeastern Idaho. I cannot tell you where this place is if I value my life but I can tell you that it is a boom or bust type area for birds with drought years being worth avoiding. A landowner was at the bar and had been drinking heavily—he was talking to the owner and sounded upset. For some reason he came over to our table and visited with us to let off steam. He had given a couple of guys permission to hunt on his land but came back to find those guys and a very large group of their friends (over 20 people total) hunting. It is understandable that he would be upset. I'm sure he would have let us hunt after we had visited. I can assure you, if we had hunted his land there would have been no extra hunters other than the three of us. We tried to tell him that most hunters would not bring back a crowd but I'm guessing the large group of hunters had done damage to future hunter access on that land. Next time he allows hunters, I'm betting he makes it clear not to bring a bunch of others.

When I take friends hunting on private lands on which I have obtained permission, it is normally with the understanding that they will not go back unless they go with me. The same gentleman's agreement stands when I go hunting on private land that someone else has obtained permission to hunt. This hunter's agreement greatly reduces a common problem of people going back with their friends and soon bringing a crowd. In the latter case, the landowner can feel overrun and begin to wonder why he ever allowed hunting in the first place. And, you will then regret sharing this hunting spot with the friend.

The only time I recall getting into trouble with a landowner over bird hunting was over a time-of-day misunderstanding. The landowner had given me permission to hunt with two friends on his place but I had mistakenly thought I could hunt all day. Instead, he expected me to be done within a few hours and had given someone else the right to hunt that evening. I did not listen carefully when I asked for permission and I was very embarrassed to have made that mistake. My apology was accepted but I still regret making that error.

When hunting private property, remember to leave the gates as they are, stay clear of buildings and cattle, pick up litter (yours and others), and otherwise be courteous. It is great if you get to know the landowner and family and develop a trust and friendship. Some hunters get involved in helping on the farm to fix fences, put in wildlife food plots, clear dead wood, or otherwise provide a hand. You will very likely end up with life long friends if you return on a regular basis. I know a few landowners well enough that I would certainly hope they would visit and stay with us if they come to Utah. I have made that invitation clear.

The best time to get permission to hunt is before the season or even after the season during some late winter cottontail hunting. Lots of landowners like having you help reduce the cottontail population in their shelterbelts. You can make some good friends cottontail hunting while helping reduce damage sometimes caused by these bunnies. Eastern cottontail hunting is usually very good in the brushy shelterbelts in eastern South Dakota.

The opening weekend or week of pheasant season is a time often reserved for family or friends so it is probably not the most opportune time to be seeking permission. Some parts of the state with unusually high pheasant populations can be more difficult for getting permission than other less known areas. In popular pheasant areas you will run into more fee access type hunting or even commercial preserves but the landowners are still usually friendly. It does not hurt to courteously ask. The biggest problem in getting permission can be finding the landowner, particularly with the increase in absentee landowners.

When you meet private landowners, it can become much more than just a hunt. The people, the land, the farmstead, the wildlife, become integrated into your life, woven into the fiber of your existence and of your memories.

Ch. 12. Tribal lands

South Dakota has extensive areas of tribal land that can be great hunting for upland game birds. Tribal lands have their own natural resource agencies and sell their own hunting licenses for those lands. They also have their own season dates. Upland bird licenses are very reasonably priced. Places like Lower Brule Indian Reservation, Standing Rock Indian Reservation, Cheyenne River Indian Reservation, Rosebud Indian Reservation, Pine Ridge Indian Reservation and other smaller Indian reservations can have great upland bird hunting. The landscapes on these reservations are often dominated by grass-forb cover that provides nesting and brood rearing habitat for prairie grouse and pheasants. Be sure to know the boundaries when hunting on land near Indian reservations (and vice versa) since state hunting licenses do not cover hunting on reservations and reservation licenses do not cover hunting on non reservation lands.

I observed the highest densities of sharp-tailed grouse I have ever observed in the mid or late 1990s (can't remember the year) while driving through the Cheyenne River Indian Reservation. I had to slow down for much of the drive to avoid having a grouse come through my windshield. I observed hundreds of sharp-tailed grouse and many pheasants in a half hour period of driving within the reservation. I'm sure grouse populations that year were unusually high. I did hunt Lower Brule Indian Reservation for a couple of days in the mid 1970s and got dog points on good numbers of sharp-tailed grouse, greater prairie-chickens, and ring-necked pheasants. Check the Internet for hunting opportunities and costs on Indian Reservations in South Dakota. In planning a reservation hunt, be sure to determine if a guide is required or if you can hunt without a guide.

Ch. 13. Fee access lands and commercial (licensed) pheasant preserves

This book is written mostly for hunters with gun dogs planning to hunt on their own on public lands, on private lands open to foot access (walk-in areas), or on private land by permission of the landowner. However, if you have the funds, both fee access and commercial pheasant preserves can offer good pheasant hunting. Fee access areas are simply private lands where the landowner allows hunting of primarily wild-hatched pheasants for a specific amount per hunter per day. An example might be $50.00 or $100 per day per hunter. Paying an access fee can be a good way to secure excellent hunting with minimal competition. On fee access areas you will be on your own so this type of hunt would appeal to hunters who have bird dogs and who like to hunt alone or with a few friends.

Commercial pheasant preserves can offer excellent pheasant hunting over an extended season. Most advertise over the Internet. Some of the larger preserves with extensive habitat have lots of wild pheasants (hatched and reared in the wild by a wild hen pheasant) to go along with released pheasants. Many of the commercial pheasant preserves release fully colored cock pheasants just prior to hunts to assure hunter success. Guides and dogs are usually provided on the larger pheasant preserves. Hunting on pheasant preserves can be expensive but success is usually assured and other amenities are provided on the more expensive hunts. Other amenities could include a guide, hunting dogs, bird processing, excellent food, a hunting lodge, showers, and a place to bunk.

If you have your own gun dog and you arrange a hunt on a commercial pheasant preserve, make sure you will not be expected to hunt with strangers or with a group of five or six hunters or more. If you own a gun dog and want to hunt alone or with a friend and without a guide, be sure to call ahead and make sure this arrangement is acceptable.

Part III. Hunting the wily ringneck—challenges and tips

Ch. 14. Roosters, roosters, and more roosters

In this section I share tips and experiences that have helped me successfully hunt pheasants in South Dakota over the past 41 years. Our home in Brookings was almost two hours' drive (four hours from the best areas) from productive spots for prairie grouse so by necessity I spent most of my time pursuing pheasants. Hunting close to home was also plenty important in terms of work, family, and finances.

The numbers of hunters pursuing pheasants in South Dakota far exceed the numbers hunting prairie grouse. Thus, in seeking an audience for this book I have recognized that interested readers will primarily be pheasant hunters or potential pheasant hunters. For this reason, the book is somewhat heavier in its coverage of pheasant hunting than for prairie grouse. In truth, I love pursuing sharp-tailed grouse and greater prairie-chickens every bit as much as hunting pheasants. All of these birds are great species for working your gun dogs and your legs.

Since retiring and moving to Springville, Utah, in the summer of 2003, my hunting in South Dakota has been much more evenly distributed between hunting prairie grouse and pheasants. To accomplish this I have increased the proportion of hunting time spent in counties near the Missouri River. These central (on an east-west axis) South Dakota counties generally have a higher percentage of grasslands than most eastern counties and often support, along with ring-necked pheasants, greater prairie-chickens (more central and southern counties near the Missouri River), and sharp-tailed grouse.

Ch. 15. The Corn harvest—better than opening day

It was a dark day in early November with what looked like an incoming storm. It could have started raining hard any time and I had already felt a few light sprinkles. I was planning to hunt on private land around a large wetland with a wide strip of unmowed and ungrazed grass-forb cover next to a broad strip of cattails and phragmites. There was open water in the more central portions of the wetland and I knew that flocks of ducks would be flushing or landing periodically as I hunted the periphery. The area was about 25 miles west of Brookings. I have known Buddy and Gwen since I approached them to ask permission to hunt at least 20 years ago. I know this family well enough that I stop by and visit when I get to South Dakota even if I'm not planning to hunt. When I hunted there in 2013 they sent me home with two quart jars of honey produced by honey bees kept on their land.

Peripheral to the main wetland were two cornfields that were being harvested; adjacent to this private land on two sides were two large Waterfowl Production Areas. If needed, I could move between the private and public land since I shoot only steel shot (required on most public lands). I knew the hunting for the next several days was likely to be better than on opening day because of the recent and ongoing harvest of surrounding cropland. Plenty of pheasants had likely flown out of the newly harvested corn into the grass and wetland cover I was planning to hunt.

I roughly followed my Brittany as she worked the edge of the grass and cattails and repeatedly trailed pheasant scent into the dense cover. The birds were smart and hard to hold but periodically my dog froze on point and I got ready for pheasants to rocket out of the cover. The hunting was good, and in less than three hours I had a limit of three roosters despite missing shots on a couple of others. As I approached the road a black SUV with Iowa plates and four hunters approached. They could see that I had been successful by the tail feathers sticking out of my hunting vest and stopped to chat, clearly anxious for some tips on how to hunt pheasants.

These Iowa hunters had not flushed many pheasants and their dreams of success were fading. This was probably their first South Dakota hunt and I figured they needed a boost of optimism. I suspected they had mostly been driving around looking for a spot that looked good. Like many hunters visiting South Dakota, they had probably heard misleading stories of myriads of pheasants flushing everywhere—they were learning. I told them the hunting was excellent if they would get their hunting dogs into the cover and work hard. They had two black Labradors that would likely do a good job finding the birds. They told me it was difficult to find a good place to hunt and I told them they had plenty of good hunting available on thousands of acres of nearby public land even without finding a landowner to get permission.

I suggested they look around and note the corn that was being harvested. Farmers were anxious to get the corn harvested before what looked like an incoming storm. In fact, you could hear a combine nearby and I could occasionally see it when it crossed a higher point of land. I pointed them to the two large federal Waterfowl Production Areas (WPAs) next to where I was hunting and told them the newly cut corn will have forced good numbers of largely unhunted pheasants into the adjacent cover on public land. All these hunters had to do was to get their dogs out and start walking the upland and wetland cover on these public areas or one of the many other public areas within a few miles. Over 5,000 acres of public hunting land existed within 10 miles of the spot I was parked. Very few of these public areas were likely being hunted that day despite it being only about two weeks after the opener. The guys were appreciative and headed off to start serious hunting. I was positive they would find some roosters and successfully harvest birds if they were willing to work hard. Their Labrador retrievers should have been plenty efficient at finding pheasants, flushing them, and retrieving downed birds. These hunters just needed to know the relationship between crop harvest and some of the best pheasant hunting of the year.

A few years ago I was traveling to Brookings after hunting near Gettysburg and Mobridge on walk-in areas (leased public access) and on public lands along or within several miles of the Missouri River. Hunting had been terrific all week and I had limited on sharp-tailed grouse and pheasants earlier that day with lots of beautiful points by my dog. I stopped in Aberdeen at a convenience store and asked two "lost looking" 50- to 60-year-old hunters how they were doing. They were from Michigan on their first South Dakota hunt and were discouraged, having almost no success after a couple of days of hunting. They were experienced upland game hunters and were hunting over a good Labrador retriever on private land near Aberdeen, an area with substantial numbers of pheasants in most years. They looked tired and especially discouraged. They asked me about my own success and were surprised by my positive results on pheasants and grouse. Their words of "can you help us" left an impression in my mind.

I knew it had been an extremely wet summer and fall and that most the corn around Aberdeen had not yet been harvested. Farmers would need to wait for the corn to dry and the ground to freeze to get into most of the fields. Many of the birds were staying in the uncut crops to feed and to avoid hunting pressure until moving into grassland roosting areas late in the day, often after sunset. Also, many chicks had died in the unusually cool and wet brood rearing period and pheasant numbers were down from normal in that area. My suggestion to these two hunters was to move their hunt 50 to 100 miles farther west, closer to the Missouri River, or even to spots west of the Missouri river where the climate is drier and where crop harvest had already taken place or was underway. I don't know how they did but I do know that this strategy can work very well for getting into the birds. Winter and spring wheat, common in counties closer to the Missouri River, are early harvested crops. Harvest of other crops, such as corn and sunflowers, is also usually earlier in drier, more western parts of the South Dakota pheasant range.

Finding Paradise in South Dakota

In 2013 pheasant projections based on brood surveys were poor for South Dakota. In addition to lower than normal pheasant populations, fall rains and early snows caused the crop harvest to be later than normal. However, for those who hunted after crop harvest the results greatly improved. In one case I was told the bird populations were dismal in the area I was hunting south of Brookings. I then hunted some private land where the corn was cut on the previous day and limited on roosters in less than an hour and a half. Later in the season I heard plenty of great reports from friends during this supposedly "dismal" pheasant year. Hunting after the crops are harvested, especially in the immediate week of post crop harvest, can change average or poor pheasant hunting into dynamite hunting. It can also improve the prairie grouse hunting.

When crops such as corn, sunflowers, or sorghum are being harvested, pheasants using these fields for feeding can often be observed flying out of croplands and into more huntable cover. If you are lucky enough to find this active crop harvest situation, these birds are usually a bit more naïve and can provide great work for the dogs. Be on the lookout during late October and early November for harvesting equipment in action near good cover on public hunting lands, walk-in areas, or private lands. It is the perfect hunting situation for wild pheasants.

After crops are harvested and for the remainder of the season pheasants spend much more of their time in protective grass-forb cover on nearby uplands or in other cover such as wetland vegetation. Sometimes, as you stop the car or get out of the vehicle, pheasants feeding in harvested crops on private land will fly out of the cropland and directly into the adjacent grass-forb cover you may be planning to hunt. In late October in 2011 I drove out to some private areas near Pierre that were leased by the South Dakota Department of Game, Fish and Parks as public walk-in areas for pheasants early in the season and as goose hunting areas later in the year. I had already hunted with my dog for two hours and had not bagged a single pheasant. As I pulled up to look at a walk-in area I watched as multiple pheasants flew from adjacent corn that was actively being harvested into the grass and cattail cover along a drainage ditch I planned to hunt.

Thank you, thank you! Less than two hours later I had taken a limit of roosters, all over points by my Brittany.

Look for attractive grass-forb cover or wetland cover on walk-in areas, public land such as a state Game Production Area or federal Waterfowl Production Area, or on private land (only with permission, of course). If the adjacent crop has just been harvested or is being harvested, the hunting can be like a second opening day except with little or no competition from other hunters. I prefer the post-harvest week of hunting over the opening day or week by far. Actually, I must confess, I prefer any week of hunting pheasants over the first week of the general season.

This walk-in area (a 200 yard wide grass and cattail strip) and ongoing corn harvest in an adjacent field made for a memorable day and easy dog points on roosters.

Ch. 16. Wild and tricky ringnecks—run, run, run, runaway

There was about five inches of new snow on the ground and it was mid-November in the early 1980s. I was hunting for pheasants near Brookings along the north side of a largely abandoned railroad northwest of Volga. My Brittany, Rascal, was hot on bird scent picked up only about 200 yards from the car and I could periodically see single pheasant tracks where they were not concealed by the vegetation and snow canopy. I was surprised to see so few tracks but I assumed most of the pheasants were on the opposite side of the railroad right-of-way in a large, densely vegetated wetland that I planned to hunt later. Based on size of the single tracks, it was a rooster. Even when I could not see tracks I knew the bird was running ahead based on the dogs actions. I suspected this bird had some experience with dogs, hunters, and snow. Rascal kept on the scent of this rooster. I moved along fast, following the dog as she made several brief points, each time deciding the bird had moved.

I had walked almost a mile in the cover next to the railroad before the dog locked up on a solid point. The pheasant probably held because of the section line road that we were approaching. I walked up to my pointing Brittany and flushed a particularly colorful adult rooster in easy range. Cock pheasants always seem especially colorful when snow blankets the ground and vegetation. I could tell this rooster pheasant was at least 16 month old from the long, adult shaped spurs (see *Ring-necked Pheasants: Thriving In South Dakota*, pg. 24). It had given us a real run. Had the rooster not been limited by the 40-yard wide piece of cover and adjacent tilled field (no cover) along the north side of the railroad, I doubt that we would have stuck with the chase. I don't often trail a single bird this far nor would I know it was the same bird except for the new snow and clearly visible single tracks along much of the way. It gives me clear evidence of how far some pheasants will run to avoid a hunter.

Most pheasants flush wild, evade the dog in other ways, or hold for the point before running this far but they can be long-distance runners. My experience is that wild hatched and wild reared pheasants are crazy runners most of the time. New snow can help slow them but that did not work in this case. It reminds me of a popular song by Del Shannon when I was a teenager in Coos Bay Oregon in the late 1950s that had the words "run, run, run, runaway, my little runaway"—ring-necked pheasants fit that song. They are a great challenge for a hunter over a gun dog.

Today the legality of access to some railroad rights-of-way is in question but in the 1970s and 1980s I found plenty of pheasants along railroads.

Wild pheasants are crazy runners! (Courtesy of Bob Hodorff)

Ch. 17. Outfoxing wily roosters

Lands open to public access such as Game Production Areas (state), Waterfowl Production Areas, and walk-in areas in portions of the state such as near Interstate 90 in central South Dakota can get substantial hunting pressure at least on the opening weekend. Still, when I have stopped to hunt these more heavily hunted areas after the first few weeks of the season I found plenty of pheasants, but the trick is to outsmart them. You can also often hear multiple roosters crowing on these public access areas if you are hunting near sunset or if you just hang around and listen at these heavily hunted sites near sunrise or after sunset. The cackling after sunset can be impressive!

For example, I sometimes hunt near Vivian (west of Chamberlain) on public areas or walk-in areas that get heavy pressure early in the season. For pheasants, I usually make sure the area or part of the area has approximately knee-high cover or taller of adequate density for the birds to find concealment. Such areas often hold abundant pheasants and sometimes have greater prairie-chickens and sharp-tailed grouse. In these heavily hunted areas my dog finds hot pheasant scent almost always within a few minutes after leaving the vehicle. The problem in getting close to experienced pheasants is that they are just too accomplished at evading people, mostly by running or flushing out of range. Wild pheasants can even be tricky on the first day of the general season or even on the earlier three-day resident-only season (held on public access lands). I enjoy hunting these extra wild birds in more heavily hunted areas because of the challenge. Hunters will never push most of these pheasants out of these areas open to public access—deep snow covering and flattening the grass-forb cover can push them out.

My most effective trick on these heavily hunted areas is to push running pheasants (what other kind is there) toward a corner or edge bordered by roads, harvested crops, heavy cover along streams (or any similar kind of linear cover), cattail stands of any kind, or some other habitat that will often cause birds to hold. This is basically psyching the birds out. If you have two hunters with dogs this method can work especially well by having both hunters push toward a corner or other spot where pheasants are likely to hold for a few minutes. In such areas I will start a push of these elusive birds toward such a corner (or holding spot) a few hundred yards or more ahead.. Since you are hunting the area anyway, you might as well push toward cover or edges where the birds are more likely to hold. Be especially ready when you get close to the corner or habitat edge! You can also hunt grassland cover parallel to a gravel road or harvested field so you at least have a border that can encourage some birds to hold. Even if some pheasants are holding for you without use of edges or corners, it pays to push toward these holding spots when the opportunity arises. Small streams or drainages with cattail stands can be great spots for getting running pheasants that would otherwise keep moving to stop and hold in the cover.

On a friends private land in northern South Dakota I stopped to hunt an area with over a section of Conservation Reserve land. It was mid November in the late 1990s and there was no snow. As I stepped out of the vehicle and shut the door, nervous pheasants started flying out of the cover hundreds of yards ahead of me in the area I planned to hunt. They definitely had the willies and flushing birds made others take flight. The dog and I pushed east into the cover, further making the field come alive as birds flew well in advance of our approach. So many birds, such great cover, such nervous birds! The number of birds was an incredible sight that I can picture to this day. I'm guessing I counted over 300 pheasants flushing ahead of me by time I had walked 300 yards and, if I recall correctly, only a couple of hens held on point. This was one of those unusual days and places where the pheasants were as thick as some of the South Dakota tales would make people expect far too often. The wildness of the birds, well that is a behavior to be expected.

I decided to swing slightly back to the north and then back northwest toward where there was a corner bordered by a county road and a tilled field. Although I saw fewer birds than at first, birds were still bursting into flight out of range or running in front of me. Many of the birds that flushed landed before the county road and tilled field ahead. Running birds and those that landed clearly wanted to avoid crossing the open of the imposing road and tilled field. As I approached within 100 yards of the corner my Brittany started getting solid points on pheasants. I knew we had made the right move by pushing for the corner. Numerous hens and several gorgeous roosters held for me in a few acres of the drab, gray, exotic bromegrass near that corner.

I'm always amazed how the brilliantly colored cock pheasants can hide so close to a pointing dogs nose and suddenly come rocketing out of the grasses. You can almost never spot the hidden roosters on the ground even with the brilliant reds, bright greens, and the white neck collar. Their colors are much more camouflaging in nature than one would think. The shooting was soon over. It was a memorable spot and one of those times I should have packed the camera. I finished the day watching the dog point a few more pheasants near my feet and enjoying seeing the colors of the hens and roosters as they skied just a few yards from the dog. Cluck, cluck, cluck, cluck, cluck! That clucking rooster sound stays in my memories as does the vision of that great day and so many great days in South Dakota.

Suddenly rocketing out of the cover! (Courtesy of Bob Hodorff)

Ch. 18. Wide ranging pointing dogs and heavily hunted roosters

Hunters with wide-ranging pointers may find good success by letting the dog range and getting points on running pheasants at a considerable distance. Many pointers get quite good at this. During a snowless year on the last day of the season (around the early 1980s) I was working my Brittany Pepsi on a federal Waterfowl Production Area (WPA) about 20 miles southwest of Brookings (near Nunda) and I needed one more pheasant to fill out. The pheasants were present in good numbers but were running like elusive late-season pheasants usually run when there is no snow cover. They all seemed to be track stars in sprint events. Pepsi was hot on birds most of the time and they were running her in wide circles. I knew my best chance to get that last rooster was to push toward some kind of habitat border or let the dog range far ahead of me and hope she could pin down a rooster. On this particular WPA I could see my dog at a considerable distance so I let her range much farther than normal (usually about 40 or 50 yds.) to try and get that last bird. She trailed hot pheasant scent all over the flats and hillsides at a considerable speed and I was about to call her back in when she went on solid point on an adjacent slope over 200 yards away. I hurried over to her thinking the pheasant would flush before I could get there but it held tight. I ended the season with a close shot over a classic dog point on a well-educated, adult ring-necked pheasant.

If the cover is such that I can see the dog regularly, I like letting a pointer cover lots of territory well out of gun range to hold these running pheasants. The method works especially well for sharp-tailed grouse and greater prairie-chickens in mixed-grass prairie habitats.

Ch. 19. Late afternoon through sunset—the magic hours

On the opening Saturday of pheasant season a few of the larger public hunting areas in southeastern South Dakota's best pheasant counties can look pretty crowded with parking lots filling up with vehicles well before shooting hours (noon). In contrast, later in the afternoon, most of the hunters will have shot their limit or, more likely, bagged one or two birds and given up for the day. Late in the afternoon is also the time when pheasants in unharvested cropland on surrounding private lands begin flying back into public areas to get ready for roosting. You can often hear the roosters cackling as they fly back into the public area or as they interact with each other on the ground. If it is a dark cloudy day the pheasants will move back to this roosting cover even earlier.

Even on more lightly hunted public areas in lower density pheasant country, early season pheasant hunting gets especially good later in the day. Again, this is particularly true on darker days. Pheasants moving into night roosting cover also often hold better for dogs than birds earlier in the day. Late afternoon movements into roosting cover (grass-forb cover) are most pronounced when the adjacent crops are still standing and have provided the birds with daytime refuge and feeding. This can also be true for sharp-tailed grouse and greater prairie-chickens.

In early November I was hunting near Pierre on several walk-in areas. Earlier in the week, I had avoided these areas because they were getting quite a bit of hunting pressure. I had hunted hard earlier in the afternoon with no luck other than flushing a few hens on point and a few roosters that flushed out of good range. With a little more than an hour before sundown I checked another leased public access hunting area where over 100 acres of knee-high grass cover bordered a standing cornfield. The bottomland was a large, almost dry wetland (just a little muddy) with extensive cattails and clumps of phragmites. Pheasants from the standing corn would likely start moving into

Finding Paradise in South Dakota

the grass and wetland cover to get ready for night roosting. As I was looking at the area, a group of five roosters from the standing corn glided into the roosting cover less than 75 yards away. Grabbing my dog and shotgun I headed for these birds—five smart rooster. I ended up flushing five roosters within 80 yards of where the group landed, passing up marginal shots because not one of them held for a close-up dog point. If these five had flown in during that short period there should be many more in the grass or soon to arrive from the cornfield.

Ten minutes later a single rooster held tight for a point in the edge of the grass where it abutted against harvested wheat—one rooster down. Moving next into the cattails in the bottomland I soon finished out on pheasants over points by my Brittany and watched the dog point two other roosters within five yards of me plus multiple hens on the way back to the vehicle. This popular spot was hot because of the timing—the birds were moving into roosting cover from standing cropland as evening approached.

A few miles west of Brookings, low, dark clouds and the year's first snow had moved in on this early November day (early 1990s)—the darkness felt like some foreboding omen of a coming disaster. The darkness belied that it was still 30 minutes before sunset and the end of shooting hours. In the falling snow under black storm clouds my dog pointed multiple roosters and hens that had moved into roosting cover and I experienced good hunting and several flushes close to my feet. Even though I thought I could tell some of the cocks from hens in the unusual darkness of the storm, the birds I shot were those that cackled to provide additional confirmation of their sex. From our studies on radio-transmitted pheasants I knew these flushed birds would land again and roost in the large Conservation Reserve field and I was not worried about influencing their survival as they faced the oncoming storm—at least other than the two I took home.

Hunting late in the day, especially in the first few weeks of the pheasant season, is always a good trick to remember to increase your success. Early in the season, I often rushed out for a one- or two-hour late afternoon pheasant hunt when I lived in Brookings.

This favorite spot south of Brookings had dense wetland cover, planted native grasses, and nearby cropland. It was a great place for a late afternoon pheasant hunt.

Rascal after a dynamite evening hunt in the late 1980s.

Ch. 20. A freshly fallen snow

Late in November, Dale Gates and I drove about 25 miles northwest of Brookings to hunt pheasants on a public area dominated by a mostly dry 10-acre wetland. It was a Saturday in the late 1970s or early 1980s. About five inches of new snow was draped over the dense wetland cover, the weight having a flattening effect. With the first snow of the year, pheasants, especially the juveniles (most already fully colored), are often a bit confused and will hold for point much better than normal. This wetland had good stands of river bulrush along with a variety of other plants (drawdown plants) that had sprung up on the moist soil. As we pushed through the snow and cover, our two Brittanys kept pointing pheasants that were holding tight under the snow cover. The number of birds holding in this small marsh was difficult to believe and the dogs got about 40 points on tight holding pheasants during the day. Most were hens but we eventually pinned down several of the more elusive roosters. Thanks to patience, new snow, and hunting dogs it had been a great day for pheasant hunting.

It was in the mid-1980s in November and overnight the first storm of the winter season dumped about 6 inches of snow across the landscape. After my 2:00 p.m. lecture, I grabbed my Brittany Rascal, and headed to a favorite spot of private land about 20 miles south of Brookings. I worked plenty of nights and Saturdays at the university so I had no problems planning ahead for some free time during pheasant season.

With the new snow I knew the birds would have moved into heavier cover, primarily around the wetlands but also in taller grass and forb cover. Rascal and I started working along the edge of a cattail-choked wetland. Multiple pheasant tracks and Rascals actions told me we were close to birds. She worked the cover hard and pointed two hens before finding a rooster. I had to almost kick the rooster to get it out of the cover but I was not surprised as pheasants in new snow often hold incredibly tight. Against the snow, cattails, and cold gray sky the colorful rooster exploded up out of the cattails in good range. After a nice retrieve, I moved on. With the new snow, pheasant hunting and a limit of birds that day would be easier than normal.

For pheasant hunting you can't beat new snow, fresh tracks, and dense wetland cover. (Courtesy of Andy Gabbert)

My experience is that gun dogs can more easily pass up holding pheasants that have moved under a snow canopy than under regular conditions. In some situations it is quite open underneath the vegetation or at least enough so for the pheasants to move about. How do I know there is open space under some snow canopies? I know because as a hunter as well as a pheasant researcher I sometimes get down close to the ground to look at habitats from the pheasants view point. Of course, I may look pretty silly doing this, especially when I'm crawling on my belly under the snow and overhead vegetation—I sometimes look a bit like a snowman when I emerge.

Finding Paradise in South Dakota

Pheasants under the snowy cover make for a unique but really enjoyable hunt. Ring-necked pheasants, exploding from new snow cover, snow flying in all directions, brilliant colors in the sun—life is good on a South Dakota pheasant hunt in new snow. When pheasants flush really close, be sure to wait a second on the shot so you do not damage the meat too much. I have so many memories of these moments—gun dogs, pheasants, new snow, and friends.

Dense wetland cover (bottomland), planted grassland, and nearby corn (narrow strip left unharvested) make this a terrific spot to hunt after a new snow. (Courtesy of Andy Gabbert)

Ch. 21. But someone just hunted that spot

It was the last weekend of the South Dakota pheasant hunting season sometime in the late 1970s and, as usually happens on a beautiful final Saturday, quite a few hunters were out. The season at that time ended around the first weekend in December. About three inches of snow had fallen the night before and temperatures were close to freezing with minimal wind—perfect pheasant hunting weather. That day I had headed to public Game Production Areas (GPAs) and Waterfowl Production Areas (WPAs) south of Lake Poinsett and about 30 miles northwest of Brookings. I knew that public areas with good winter cover could be excellent hunting late in the year. I arrived at about 1 p.m. and the first public area I checked had at least two parties already hunting. I checked a second area, a WPA, and saw two hunters with dogs just exiting some of the heavier cover and walking back up to their vehicle. This area was fairly small, maybe about 100 acres. The 10 acres of frozen wetland in the middle had large patches of dense cattail cover and picked corn was evident on private land nearby. I assumed it had been fairly well hunted by the two hunters and their gun dogs.

I was thinking I would look elsewhere for a place that had not been hunted when I saw a rooster pheasant glide into the dense cattail cover in the frozen wetland. The two departing hunters were still on the area but were unaware of the rooster that had landed about 200 yards behind them. As the other hunters departed I took my Brittany and headed into the dense wetland cover.

Reaching the area where I had seen the rooster land, Pepsi picked up hot scent. We started working birds and the pheasants did their part to make the hunt challenging. After about 30 minutes Pepsi got a rooster to hold for a close shot. Of course, I had no idea if it was the same bird I had seen fly into the cattails. Not wanting to try and find another spot, and enjoying the hunt, I decided to just stay at this spot for a while. Pheasant tracks in the fresh snow that occasionally crossed my tracks, the tracks of the other hunters, or fresh dog tracks convinced me more pheasants were simply evading me and running ahead and around me in circular patterns in the cattail cover. Pepsi kept working birds through the afternoon and I just enjoyed watching her work with no concern about getting more birds. That day I spent my entire hunt on a wetland that had already been hunted before me (that same day) by people with hunting dogs. An hour before sunset I shot my third rooster, the last bird for the season.

Further evidence that small areas that have already been hunted that day by you or others can still produce birds accumulated over the years. Pheasants often run ahead and circle in good cover and some of them stay to say bon voyage as hunters and dogs come and go during the day. Most experienced hunters will remember searching hard for a downed pheasant and getting a point on a different rooster that was in the same cover already searched a couple of times—obviously some of these birds escape detection by experienced gun dogs.

South of Gettysburg, Dale Gates and I hunted a large walk-in-area grassland in early November in the early 2000s where Dale had been successful earlier in the season. The week-old snow was at least six inches deep and the birds were bunched up and especially nervous in the cover of intermediate wheatgrass. We could see little in the way of really heavy cover such as dense cattails or weed stands. With the exception of a few hens that held tight, pheasants were flushing in good numbers far ahead of our two Brittanys. After about two hours, we were about to give up on the area but spotted a dense, linear stand of cattails (and some phragmites) in a deep draw along a small intermittent stream. The stand was only about 30 yards long and 5 or 6 yards wide. As we walked toward the patch of cover, at least 35 pheasants with good numbers of roosters exploded into to the air while we were still over 80 yards away. There seemed little chance of getting closer and we were frustrated with the situation. Still, we moved ahead to see if a couple of birds had stayed in the heavy cover. We walked the dogs through the two dense stands of cattails and phragmites with no luck. All the birds had flushed wild!

Dale moved up the streambed to another site with some cover. Although I also felt there were no birds remaining in this 30 yard, linear cover patch and was ready to move on, my dog did not agree and went back to work the cover further. She had proven me wrong before. Brook just kept working the small area of cover until, almost unnoticed by a disbelieving me, she froze up on solid point and a cock subsequently skied into the air out of the tall phragmites where it had held tight. I was so surprised that I missed an easy shot and while bemoaning that fact lost track of the dog. Looking around I found she was again on tight point in the same small patch of heavy cover. That rooster was not so lucky! Pheasants can hold tight and bird hunting can still be good even after you or others have worked cover with experienced dogs or after you have watched most of the pheasants flush well ahead of your dog.

This phragmites (common reed) is around 7 feet tall and quite dense. Pheasants commonly skyrocket into the air when flushed from this tall wetland cover.

Ch. 22. Poor pheasant year—why show up?

My wife's parents, Ruel and Beth Allen, would visit us from Logan Utah each fall when we lived in Brookings. Of course the fall visit was timed so Ruel could pursue pheasants for a few weeks. Sometimes I think my Brittanys recognized Ruel and not me as the best bet for getting in more hunting time. We hunted about 20 years together before his death at 70 years old of a heart attack while helping move a piano for a widow in his Logan neighborhood. A few months earlier I had tried to stop Ruel from running after a downed pheasant in a harvested cornfield because of my concerns about triggering a heart attack. I clearly recall yelling "let the dog get it Ruel." Ruel was a great hunting buddy, grandfather to our children, and dear friend. Pretty lucky in terms of finding the right father-in-law.

One day in the mid to late 1970s Ruel went downtown in Brookings to get shotgun shells at the local sporting goods store and talked to the owner Bob Wakeman. Bob knew plenty about pheasants and he gave people an honest evaluation about their probable success hunting local areas. The word was out that brood counts were much lower than normal in Brookings and nearby counties and that it was not a good place to try and get birds. Even most of the locals were avoiding Brookings County and surrounding areas and instead hunting an hour to two hours west where pheasants were more abundant. I cannot recall why the counts were so low but I believe it was due to local drought conditions affecting nesting or to an unusually severe winter.

Bob knew Ruel was a nonresident and would struggle finding birds locally, so he told him he needed to head west at least 100 miles to get into decent numbers of pheasants. He told Ruel he would be wasting his time to hunt pheasants in or near Brookings County. Bob asked Ruel if he was hunting with anyone and Ruel gave him my name. Knowing that I was an avid pheasant hunter and knew the area, Bob then told Ruel "to forget everything I just told you." That gave me some added prestige with my father-in-law but it was really something Bob would have said if a nonresident were going with a number of other hunters that he knew to be well experienced with the local area and with pheasants. No, Bob and I did not plan that out to give me points with my in-laws.

Even during bad years in the worst counties, there are hot spots. People who know the county can probably find good hunting. Bob knew I would take Ruel to areas that had birds. He also knew I had a good hunting dog and that there are always more birds out there than people think. Ruel and I did just fine that year and, because so many people avoided these areas of "predicted low pheasant numbers," we found an unusually high ratio of roosters to hens. In fact, on many public areas, the number of roosters flushed was almost equal to the number of hens even after the second and third weeks of the season. There were simply no people hunting on most days and plenty of pheasants had not even encountered hunters.

Even in the traditionally lower-density pheasant spots in the state, hunters can usually find decent pheasant hunting if they know pheasant habitat and if they have a good dog. Hunters in these areas are also rewarded by lack of crowding and a high ratio of roosters to hens. So don't be too concerned that hunting pheasants in the lower population years will be just terrible. Be ready to work a little harder but enjoy the lack of competition. And don't be surprised to find some "hot spots" in remote portions of the state out of the main pheasant range.

Ch. 23. Lousy looking spots could be a surprise

In central and northern portions of South Dakota, I often hunt walk-in areas because they can be great hunting and because you can hunt them without finding the landowner to get permission. Landscapes with sufficient grassland often provide good prairie grouse hunting as well as pheasant hunting. In some cases, walk-in areas may look like they have relatively sparse cover from the roadside view and are seemingly not worth hunting—from experience I can tell you some of these can be dynamite.

One of my favorite "lousy looking" walk-in areas is in western South Dakota in non traditional pheasant range. This spot brings up some great memories. It was a beautiful early November morning and I was hunting with two of my friends, Jack Connelly and Doug Finicle from Idaho. As noted in an earlier chapter, these two guys have threatened me with bodily harm if I reveal specifics about their favorite hunting areas. Even though prairie grouse are open at sunrise, we normally wait until 9 a.m. to start hunting when pheasants are open (after the first week) in South Dakota's Mountain Time zone areas. Jack and Doug both have multiple gun dogs and they start the days hunting on one of several large walk-in areas where they have had success. To keep plenty of space for the dogs I decide to check out some other walk-in areas within a mile of where Jack and Doug start hunting.

As I'm driving and looking for a promising area, five cock pheasants run out of the road ditch and into thin mixed-grass cover on a walk-in area that looks poor for attracting or holding pheasants. I watch the birds and see two of the roosters fly a few hundred yards into the walk-in area. Although I would not normally hunt such a poor-looking spot of habitat, seeing the roosters changes my mind and I head out with the dog. Traversing through the thin grass cover my dog is hot on scent. As we walk into the area I discover that the intermittent stream has considerable dense wetland cover along the edge, even including some cattail patches.

Approaching a patch of cattails along the intermittent stream close to where the roosters had flown, Brook freezes on solid point and as I approach a gorgeous rooster rises into the air at close range. As so often happens, the brilliant colors on the flushing rooster and the balancing tail feathers that seem almost too long are perfectly illuminated by the sun on the surprised and cackling rooster. I stop, enjoy the retrieve, admire the bird, and then continue to work the remainder of the intermittent stream. I finish on pheasants after watching my dog make several other close points on cocks and hens in the cattail and grass cover along the intermittent stream. Guess I will concentrate on sharptails and gray partridge for the remainder of the day. Another day in paradise!

That "lousy looking" spot has remained signed up as a walk-in area in the two other recent years I have been in the area to hunt. I have never seen another hunter on it despite the fact that hunters are commonly working nearby areas with more attractive cover. Also, since the first hunt I have followed the dog toward the back of this quarter section and have discovered additional patchy cover that is also excellent, especially an abandoned corral area near an isolated old barn that has heavy stands of kochia. The kochia (fireweed), much of it over seven feet tall, grows so well in the spot due to the rich and disturbed soils of the old corral area. Kochia provides attractive winter cover and pheasants feed on the nutritious seeds.

As I first approached this kochia stand the dog was moving cautiously, pointing, and then moving on slowly, and pointing again. I was given plenty of warning—birds just ahead! Finally, with Brook on point, over 30 pheasants flushed within 30 yards in what seemed like less than five seconds. Several roosters were within 15 yards but all flushed into the bright, blinding afternoon sun. I raised my Berretta 20 gauge and started to swing at a couple of different roosters but hesitated (due to blinding sun), and, in the end, did not fire a single shot. I clearly remember that I was shaking a bit even after all these years of hunting pheasants. What a great moment! One lesson from that event that I keep relearning—be aware of the position of the sun when the dog is hot on birds. A number of those birds did curve around and land back in the cattails along the stream as well as in a couple of other dense upland weed patches. They were pretty easy to find for the Brittany. And, oh yes, I also discovered that the lighter cover on that area was not too bad for sharp-tailed grouse and gray partridge.

Remember, walk-in areas or other lands with free public access that look poor from the road often have their rewards in the form of small, unseen wetlands (often nearly dry) with emergent cover, or other rewarding spots that are loaded with birds. I've been burned more than once with long walks and no birds but the unseen hot spots away from the road keep me walking, working the dog, and hoping to find new secret spots.

Jack Connelly's German shorthair (Gus) staunchly pointing a rooster pheasant. This favorite walk-in area for pheasants and prairie grouse looks like sparse habitat when viewed from the adjacent gravel road. (Courtesy of Jack Connelly)

My Brittany (Brook) on point in a stand of kochia.

Ch. 24. Hunting over ice—and breaking through

Pheasant hunters in East River South Dakota often find themselves hunting areas with interspersed marshes that feature dense grass, weedy cover, and sometimes sandbar willow patches around the periphery. Patches of dense cattail or other dense emergent cover in other parts of the marsh on drawdown (mudflats) or flooded areas provide valuable winter cover. These interspersed marshes are magnets for pheasants throughout the year and especially under snowy, wintery conditions. By mid November or even earlier, often before snowfall of any significance occurs, pheasants will use thin ice and emergent cover, often dense cattails, to find refuge from hunters and dogs. It can be frustrating to see the dog hot on pheasant scent and then watch as the dog attempts unsuccessfully to walk on thin ice. I have many times looked out over cattails with thin ice and have known the birds were out there but that it was either too difficult to wear hip waders and break ice or too risky to try and walk on the ice.

When I was a South Dakota resident I could plan on hunting dense winter cover on specific wetlands later in the season when the ice was adequately thick. Still, I wanted to have a good feel for the depth of the water if I did fall through. If it was only a few feet deep I was not overly concerned if I got wet. One day near Brookings I was hunting on a large semipermanent marsh on the deeper water side of a wide swath of cattails near the shoreline. I stepped on a weak spot and was immediately up to my thighs in ice water and bottom mud. Luckily I had anticipated such an event from past experience and had a set of dry clothes and hunting boots in the car a half mile from where I was hunting. However, it was a cold day with a brisk wind and when I got back to the car I was pretty solidly iced up and shivering hard. I knew the family that owned the land well and had hunted there for many years—I knew I could ask for help. At the farmhouse I was welcomed by Bob and Gladys and I changed into dry clothes and boots in the bathroom after which I was ready to hunt again.

Pheasants often move out into the cattails over ice in late fall and winter. Hunters should keep dry clothes and boots in their vehicle and avoid questionable ice where the water depth might be dangerous. (Courtesy of Kent Jensen)

    I'm sure my good friends on this farm have had to chuckle a little about that event but in deeper water it could have been a dangerous situation. I have hunted on their place for almost 40 years and they know me, they know my wife, they know my children. Likewise, I have come to know and appreciate their family. They are the sweetest of people and have become close friends, cemented by things in common and by long friendship.

    Your chances of breaking through ice are greater near or in emergent vegetation or around tiny muskrat feeder houses. These feeder houses are much smaller than the large piles of vegetation on regular muskrat houses. I recall one of our students fell through the ice while hunting pheasants where the water was at about chest level and had some difficulty getting back on the ice and making it back to his vehicle. It can be a scary and dangerous situation in deeper water. If you are hunting pheasants in South Dakota after mid November, you will likely want to hunt over ice in some situations since pheasants are attracted to the cattails and other dense emergent vegetation. Usually, cattails are located in areas of the wetland with less than two or three feet of water or even just on wet soil but keep it in mind that in some wetlands cattail patches can occur in areas with water deep enough to be a safety issue. If you know the area at all, you will know the approximate depths of water and of the unconsolidated muck under the ice and you can feel safe. You can still slip and fall on the slick ice as I have done plenty of times but for me, no broken or cracked bones yet.

Ch. 25. Winter snows, cattails, and deer trails—gut check

As the winter intensifies the snow on the uplands often blows into wetland cover. If the winter is unusually severe, drifting snow can completely fill in almost all wetland emergent cover, even to near the tops of sandbar willow clumps and tall stands of phragmites. Both the willow clumps and the phragmites can be over 10 feet tall. If this happens, pheasants are usually forced to move into farmstead woodlands and other dense tree belts of appropriate width and density. Dense emergent cover in large wetlands with unharvested corn (or other standing vegetation) on the upwind side (northwest) may be protected enough to remain available as winter habitat if the corn catches much of the drifting snow. In portions of the state that get hit with such severe winter conditions, you will seldom see a pheasant hunter and with good reason. With the deep drifting snow it is simply too tough for hunters to get around.

However, in most winters the snow remains at low or moderate depths and much of the wetland emergent cover, willow clumps, dense weed patches, and tall native grass fields such as switchgrass remain available as winter cover. The hunting in these moderate or average winter conditions can be excellent with pheasants concentrated in heavy cover and often holding tight for dogs and hunters. The experience of flushing colorful roosters in the snowy landscape is difficult to match for a pheasant hunter. If it is a dry winter with no snow, pheasant hunting is still good but the roosters can be extra tough to get close to since they are well schooled in how to elude hunters by running.

My father was in good physical shape (low body fat) but had a heavy smoking habit and died at 49—you guessed it, a heart attack; my younger brother Bob, slowed by smoking and weight, would have died at 50 except he heeded warning signs and had his massive heart attack in a Texas hospital with excellent expertise and equipment for heart problems. Bob is now much thinner and in better shape and takes great satisfaction in beating me in golf. So glad he is still around.

I have been warned that I am probably genetically vulnerable to the same heart problems so I stay clear of smoking and work at staying in good physical shape. If I have a fatal heart attack it seems appropriate that it should be while I am hunting pheasants in snow and swinging on a cackling rooster. Now that would be one of the better ways to leave this world! Of course, dragging me out would put a damper on the hunt for any hunting buddies. My hunting friend Jack Connelly assures me that dragging me out will not be a problem if the hunting is good. In that situation he stated "we may just roll you into a cattail marsh; rescue your gun, shells, and dog; then be on our way."

If you plan to hunt in late season when winter cover may have appreciable amounts of drifted snow you will need to stay in good physical shape. Your preparation for hunting heavy cover with drifted snow often over a foot deep should include regular jogging, walking, swimming, or similar activities. Hunting regularly and intensively for grouse and pheasants earlier in the season is also a good way to prepare for challenging late-season hunting.

When I was in my late 50s I vividly recall hunting an area of cattail in December that extended basically a full mile through a series of large connected marshes. The snow on the uplands was about eight inches deep but in the marsh it had drifted in to about 15-20 inches. I took a friend in his mid 30s that had asked if I he could accompany me on a late season hunt. We parked a vehicle at each end so we could hunt into the light south wind and end up at a vehicle. My friend was not overweight, but I'm sure he did not work out regularly, hunt regularly, nor had he hunted in difficult to walk snow conditions. By the time we were halfway through the hunt, it was clear he was struggling to keep up even though we were going quite slow. As I often do, we walked deer trails as much as possible through the almost solid stands of cattails.

There were plenty of pheasants and we had good opportunities. The problem was that my friend was so tired he could not keep up with the dog or with me even at a moderate or slow pace. Invariably, my Brittany, Kali, would point pheasants and they would flush too far ahead of him to get a good shot. Also, gasping for air does not help on your accuracy with a shotgun! By the time we reached the final area of heavy cattail cover near the car my friend was unable to stay mentally or physically with the hunt even though he knew we would be pushing birds into a holding spot. I continued to walk slowly through the last small wetland and its stand of heavy cattails, cornering two roosters that held for point and flushed near the end. My friend was out of breath and several yards out of range of the birds when they flushed. I had even tried unsuccessfully to flush the birds towards him. He had given up the battle. He later told me this winter pheasant hunt was the most difficult and exhausting hunt he had ever experienced. I have been told that before by hunting guests unprepared for the rigors of a late winter pheasant hunt in more than a few inches of snow.

Drifted snow in heavy cover can be a physically challenging if you are not in good condition. Don Soderlund at Sand Lake National Wildlife Refuge. (Courtesy of Don Soderlund)

I love to hunt these types of winter situations and you would love it if you have prepared yourself for these often tough walking conditions. There are almost no other hunters. The birds are all concentrated in the limited heavy cover on both public and private land. The roosters hold well for the dog in deeper snow and the colors of juvenile and adult pheasants by mid December are especially spectacular against the snowy background. Don't be worried about there not being enough pheasants for good hunting late in the season! Pheasants will usually be there in good numbers and they will be concentrated in heavy cover near agricultural food sources for some great, great hunting. This late-season hunt can be South Dakota pheasant hunting at its very best and I recommend such a hunt to any upland game hunter with the endurance, guts, and gumption to take it on.

Ch. 26. Pheasants—hanging close to food

In the fall when looking at potential pheasant spots I always look for food sources nearby. Pheasants will usually be feeding within about a half mile, often less than a quarter mile, from roosting and loafing areas. For that reason, I recommend hunting areas with waste grains or other definite food sources within this distance. Pheasants in the early fall will usually be feeding heavily on waste grains, weed seeds, a few grasshoppers, and some greens (grass, forb leaves, etc.). Occasionally I have found good numbers of pheasants a mile or more from agricultural foods that are feeding on weed seeds such as kochia or ragweed. I have even found pheasants feeding with sharp-tailed grouse in Russian olive trees with gullets full of Russian olive fruit. If there is minimal food nearby you can expect fairly low numbers of pheasants. Seeds from corn, sunflower, grain sorghum, wheat, and even soybeans are often found in the crop (gullet) of pheasants. Hunters should use the availability of both cover and food sources in picking spots to hunt.

If you see an area of upland or wetland cover suitable for pheasants with cropland nearby you can usually be confident that your gun dog will soon find fresh pheasant scent. If the cropland has been harvested it is all the better since the pheasants tend to spend more time in the huntable cover in those cases. As noted earlier, if the cropland near good cover is unharvested go ahead and hunt the adjacent cover early in the day but then plan to come back later unless you have limited out. The birds from the standing cropland will be moving back into the huntable cover in late afternoon, sometimes in large numbers.

Some of my favorite hunting spots are public or private areas next to a harvested cornfield. In eastern Brookings County, there were several large public hunting areas (WPAs and GPAs) where hunters could get a half mile from roads by walking to the back of the area. My favorite spots on those areas were sites with concealing grass or wetland cover near cut corn. Even though public, the back of these areas receive little pressure from hunters because of the required walk. In one case I had found a good spot at the back of a public area behind a large marsh but on approaching it in early season the pheasants would run into the adjacent standing corn. To get near these birds I had to walk quietly and keep my dog at heel (no talking or whistling) until I got near this site and then let her go so she could find the birds and get a solid point. If I made noise by giving commands to my dog before getting close to the spot the birds would move into the standing corn and we would find only hot scent. The trick worked great almost every time!

Harvested corn near good cover (wetland edge and dense wetland cover) usually means the dog will find fresh pheasant scent right away.

Ch. 27. Windy day birds

Most South Dakota autumn days are marked by light to moderate winds. I hope all hunters experience light winds that are perfect for working a gun dog. Nevertheless, all hunters experienced with South Dakota know that it is not unusual to spend a few days hunting in winds that are strong enough to make the hunting more challenging than normal. Such winds can occasionally even make standing upright a challenge. If the wind is moderately strong, be prepared for pheasants to run even more than usual and to be more difficult to approach within good shotgun range. This is not a scientific conclusion but simply my observation based on hunting experience. Most hunters I have talked to agree that it gets tougher when the wind gets in the 20 to 35 mile per hour range. Pheasants seem to get nervous and to run more—points and close flushes get tough. Plus, when upland birds flush in windy conditions and catch the wind it can sometimes ruin any confidence you may have built up in your wing-shooting skills.

It is also more difficult to hear a bird flush, and any upland bird hunter knows that wing sound is an important cue if the bird gets up behind you, to the side, or otherwise out of your immediate line of vision. It is also more difficult to hear cackling rooster pheasants when they flush or to hear the noisy clucking of sharp-tailed grouse. If you have hunted upland birds over gun dogs, you know the birds can be from a few yards (or less) away to out of gun range when they flush, and could be to the side or even behind you at times.

I've had some different hunting results on the days I have tried to hunt pheasants in gusting or steady winds of over 35 miles per hour. In wind at those speeds, my opinion is that the pheasants often hold fairly tight. Because of the poor flight control, they certainly do not like to take flight in extreme winds and in my opinion, running, although always a problem, is less of a problem than in moderately strong winds. Of course, hearing the bird flush or cackle is even more difficult in such extreme winds and I tend to miss more shots than normal.

On my trip to South Dakota from Utah on October 25, 2010, I stopped as I often do to stay with Mark and Kathy Rumble in Rapid City. Mark was my former graduate student at SDSU before going on for his Ph.D. at the University of Wyoming. Mark is an avid pheasant hunter and at the time had a wire-haired pointer that was an accomplished grouse and pheasant dog as well as a much loved family pet. Both he and Kathy "babied" that dog so it really got the love plus the hunting. I have stayed at their home enough that my dog Brook already knows as soon as we drive up that she is invited into the house and can be part of the evening get together.

On this particular trip, high winds were predicted the next day in advance of a large storm and low pressure system that was approaching South Dakota and Minnesota. In fact, on Tuesday, 26 October 2010, the barometric pressure in western Minnesota dropped to 28.4 inches, the lowest ever recorded. News articles on that storm and barometric low are easy to find on the Internet. That set up unusually high and sustained winds in western South Dakota where we were attempting to hunt pheasants and sharp-tailed grouse. The wind was blowing over 25 miles per hour the morning we left Mark and Kathy's home in Rapid City. We drove east to hunt in the region near Kadoka on a large walk-in area that covered a couple of sections of land (about two square miles). The area sometimes has decent numbers of pheasants and sharp-tailed grouse but is not very dependable from year to year.

Since I had to keep traveling to Brookings after the hunt, we took two vehicles across the windy plains. By time we reached the hunting area the wind had reached levels where a sane person would turn around and go home. Knowing that I had driven a long way from Utah to hunt, Mark stuck with me and we began hunting in winds of extreme speed. The wind was so ferocious that there was a constant roar or howling—you could hear almost nothing but this fearful wind. We did not at that time know we were dealing with a record setting low pressure system and the associated winds. We would later find out that peak winds reached or slightly exceeded 70 miles per hour and that sustained winds exceeded 40 miles per hour in the general region we were hunting. When walking into the most extreme gusts, you felt like you could basically lean forward as far as you wanted and the wind would hold you up. As far as hunting hats, you had better have them strapped on or they were gone.

There was no chance we could hear the flushing sound of wings, the cackling of cock pheasants, or the clucking of sharp-tailed grouse as birds got up. Even with pointing dogs, we had to be looking directly at the spot close to where the birds were hiding or we might not have time to get a shot off.

Site of the "windy day" hunt on a much calmer late October day in 2011. Mark Rumble and his wire-haired pointer (Gus) faced that "windy day" experience with me.

Mark and I headed to different parts of the walk-in area. I flushed only one rooster during about four hours of hunting and it flushed wild but, unwisely, glided into heavy cover in a draw that had some wind protection. I followed with the dog and took this rooster over a close point. Fortunately for my success, the cock flew directly into the wind, giving me a much less challenging shot than if the pheasant had flown with the wind. Sharp-tailed grouse were fairly abundant on the part of the area I hunted and, though detected and pointed within good range, invariably left me empty handed. I could not shoot in that wind and I am still wondering what the wind was doing to my shot string. At the very least it completely destroyed my confidence on that day. Mark had a similar story to tell when we got back together. Tough, tough hunt!

We stayed over at a motel in Kadoka with plans to hunt the next day. Morning arrived and the wind speed was only slightly reduced; in addition to the wind, heavy snow was now flying by in a horizontal pattern common to many storms in the plains. It was below freezing. We decided it was probably a good time to call off the hunt. I headed east to Brookings and Mark headed back to Rapid City, both of us just beating closures of Interstate 90 due to the storm and drifting snow. In a couple of days warm weather would return, the snow would melt, and hunting conditions would be back to normal.

Ch. 28. The coldest day

In the 1970s and early 1980s I would sometimes take a side trip up to Sand Lake National Wildlife Refuge (Sand Lake NWR) in northeastern South Dakota just to hunt pheasants during the refuges late season hunt (first weekend in December to the first weekend of January). The refuge was open for pheasants after the state's general pheasant season closure during those years. In more recent years the general pheasant season in the state has extended into January, so the latter part of the general season coincides with when the refuge is also open for pheasants. The refuge covers over 21,000 acres (including water bodies) and hunter density is extremely low. The refuge provides prime wintering habitat for pheasants as well as white-tailed deer. Additional public lands and walk-in areas are also found near the refuge.

This northeastern part of South Dakota can be like a cold sink when a subfreezing mass of arctic air (arctic clipper) slides down from the north. A neighbor and I had headed to Sand Lake NWR one day in late December in the early 1970s during the Christmas break at SDSU. I do not recall the year but daily high temperatures in the Aberdeen area were predicted to be barely above 0 degrees Fahrenheit with nightly lows around 20 degrees below zero. Still, we had no common sense in those days and I was sure we were tough South Dakotans and could handle the cold unless the chill factor was too high due to wind.

We arrived at Sand Lake NWR in time for the 10 a.m. start of shooting hours. We found almost no other hunters and plenty of pheasant sign (tracks) and pheasants in the dense, abundant wetland cover, primarily cattails and phragmites. However, there was a steady wind around 20 to 25 miles per hour and the cold was crippling for both of us despite wearing our version of ample winter clothing, gloves, and pull-over face masks. Looking back, we were poorly dressed for the extreme cold. After a couple of hours of hunting and some success, we found ourselves so cold we could hardly raise a shotgun on a flushing rooster even when my Brittany Pepsi had pointed a bird at close range. I recall Pepsi pointing a rooster that was holding tight within a couple of yards and finding myself so cold, bundled up, and shivering, that I just watched the flushing rooster fly off and knew he could have his freedom; I could hardly move and had had enough. So had my frozen neighbor!

As we reached the vehicles we could tell our exposed skin temperatures were at dangerous levels and our colorless noses testified that the exposed skin was freezing or had already frozen. We spent the rest of the day at the rustic and low-cost Sand Lake Motel in Hecla, before giving it one more try the next day in less windy conditions. It was still too cold but bearable. I won't attempt to define what a "rustic and low cost motel" is but hunters trying out the hunting at Sand Lake NWR should stay at this motel just for the memory.

This is the coldest hunt I can ever remember and I suspect it was a dangerous situation. Most pheasant hunters probably have better cold weather clothing than we did in the early 1970s. Still, anyone planning such a late hunt needs to be aware—hunting pheasants at these temperatures when there is an appreciable wind chill can be a special challenge. I suppose I am crazy enough to go pheasant hunting in temperatures that are below zero (or barely above zero) if there is little or no wind but I would definitely be better prepared with clothing and hand warmers this time.

Northeastern South Dakota and Sand Lake NWR are famous for these cold periods but it can also be quite warm in December and I even hunted there one snowless December when the daily temperatures reached into the 50s (Fahrenheit). It is a terrific spot for having tons of space and no competition for wild and beautiful ring-necked pheasants. I readily recommend a trip to Sand Lake National Wildlife Refuge and other nearby areas during December or early January but caution that hunters should watch and plan for periods of reasonably huntable temperatures. Or, if you're tough enough, go ahead and challenge those artic clippers! My friend Dale Gates and his French Brittanys fit the definition of tough enough. They plunged into the cold and hunted near Sand Lake NWR on walk-in areas (in the Conservation Reserve Enhancement Program) in 2013

Finding Paradise in South Dakota

during December temperatures that stayed below zero degrees Fahrenheit even at the warmest time of the day. There was no significant wind while Dale was there and he reported having no problem keeping warm. The wind chill is critical to how you can handle hunting in such cold. I'm sure he was better dressed for that kind of cold than I was during my "coldest day" hunt.

Even though 2013 was supposed to be a poor year for pheasants in South Dakota, Dale reported phenomenal pheasant hunting and easy limits every day in the Sand Lake area. And Dale Gates won't even shoot a rooster unless it holds tight on point. The hunting sounded exceptionally good and made me keep thinking about making a late season trip to the Sand Lake NWR area even though it is an 18-hour drive for me. And there would be no competition!

I tell this "coldest day" hunting story because it is one of the situations hunters could run into in a late season hunt. I also know there is good hunting on the refuge and on plenty of public land or walk-in areas near the refuge so this can be a memorable trip with premiere pheasant hunting and minimal competition from other pheasant hunters. There may be a few late season deer hunters on the refuge but that is seldom any problem.

Sand Lake National Wildlife Refuge on a snowy winter day. The pheasants have thousands of acres of protective winter cover on the refuge. (Courtesy of Don Soderlund)

Ch. 29. Hunting shelterbelts and childhood memories of an owl attack

Sometimes pheasants will be quite concentrated in shelterbelts (tree-shrub belts) during early season even though there may be good grass cover on at least one adjacent side. These birds are probably loafing under the shrubs or other cover and have moved in after feeding nearby. Some of the denser, wider shelterbelts can also harbor wintering pheasants. Shelterbelts are not a major type of cover I hunt but often make up a small part of the cover walked in a day of pheasant hunting.

It was November in the late 1970s and I was hunting a 10- to 12-row shelterbelt west of Brooking (near Sinai) that was probably planted about 30 years earlier. The grass and shrub cover underneath the trees looked good enough to hold pheasants despite the great horned owl I flushed from a tree as I walked into the belt. Seeing the great horned owl brings back memories and I think about a close encounter with this large bird when I was about 10 or 11 (early 1950s). I had found a pair of great horned owls nesting in a large stick nest built by a pair of red-tailed hawks in a previous year. The nest was in a rocky Mountain juniper tree on our farm in central Oregon. It was in my blood to find every birds nest I could and those of larger birds of prey such as red-tail hawks were good for quite the thrill since the adults would dive close to my head when I went up to look at the eggs or fuzzy young in the nest. Two of my sisters tell me I sometimes took them and encouraged them to climb the nest trees for the same experience. Sorry about that.

As I climbed the juniper to look in the owls nest, I kept a careful eye on the parents that had flown to a juniper tree about 50 yards away from me. They just sat there, hooting and staring at me—no challenge at all compared to red-tailed hawks protecting their nest. That was the case, until one of the pair flew from the perch and headed toward me and the nest. I was behind a protective limb below the nest and I felt no fear since the bird in flight looked so slow compared to diving red-tailed hawks. I should have been terrified! The owl was suddenly in my face with its sharp talons and then just as quickly had flown on. Touching my hand to my face I came back with quite a bit of blood. I quickly slid down the 20-25 feet of the large juniper, hit the ground, and ran most of the mile home. Mother looked me over: no eye damage, several surface scratches, enough blood on my face to look bad, but no need for stitches. I was lucky about the eyes and the shallow scratches. To this day I still have plenty of respect for great horned owls near their nest and the incident remains vivid in my mind. We did not have television at that time on our farm and personal computers (and computer games) were decades away but there were some real adventures out there to be had—I think I am still chasing those adventures. This particular adventure with great horned owls made a good story I often used when teaching about nest defense in birds in the ornithology class at SDSU.

Anyway, enough of the daydreaming about the owl attack and back to the business of shelterbelts and pheasants. There are lots of shelterbelts in eastern South Dakota. Some of those belts have been badly overgrazed and are not worth hunting but others have considerable grass and brush in the understory. Dense belts with outside rows of shrubs such as lilac or wild plum and with multiple rows of deciduous trees can hold pheasants if they are close to food sources. Likewise, shelterbelts with pines, spruce, and junipers can offer wind protection in winter if they contain adequate rows of trees along with shrub rows. In general, newer shelterbelts with shrub rows are the best for hunting. Food must be nearby.

The ungrazed shelterbelt where we flushed the owl featured harvested corn on one side and a lightly grazed pasture (fenced) on the other plus good numbers of pheasants in the area. My dog got hot on scent right away. After following the scent for about 200 yards she locked up on point and, as I approached, three roosters burst almost simultaneously out of the cover and almost dead center in the middle of the belt. I had considerable experience shooting at and missing pheasants where trees were in the way. I was learning that the best way to miss shots in a woodland was to try and not hit the trees. For that reason, I just forgot the trees and started swinging on the pheasants as they gained altitude through the trees. On that occasion, I remembered to ignore the trees and I bagged two of the roosters in quick succession. I have tried to remember that lesson since.

On many occasions shelterbelts have rows of junipers, pines, or spruce that can completely block your view of pheasants or grouse as they flush. The way to hunt these belts as well as many other tree belts is with one person on each side and the dog working cover inside and along the edge of the shelterbelt. In rare cases, we have placed a person on the end of the belt to block.

Young shelterbelts can hold both pheasants and prairie grouse. Dale Gates and his French Brittany (Eddy) hunt this area near the Oahe Reservoir.

Ch. 30. A list of suggestions to improve your pheasant hunting success

Herein I will attempt to list some of the approaches that can help you be successful and have a quality pheasant hunting experience in South Dakota. This list is not meant for those who like to hunt in larger groups. Most of these suggestions were included in the individual chapters in this section. If you have not hunted pheasants extensively or if you have not hunted them at all, I believe these points will help improve your success.

The pheasant list

1. A good bird dog will locate far more pheasants than you will find without a dog. It is also much more fun to hunt if you have your own gun dog. Bird dogs also reduce loss of downed birds.

2. Hunt alone or with one or two other hunters, preferably with each person having his or her own hunting dog. More than three hunters in a hunting party is a crowd in my opinion.

3. Primarily hunt dense grassland, dense weedy areas, wetland edges, or dense wetland cover (like cattails) within a half mile of cropland that produces waste grain.

4. Monitor crop harvest in planning your hunt. The best hunting with a dog is after or during harvest of fall crops, primarily corn. The opening day or week of the general pheasant opener was never my favorite time to hunt pheasants.

5. For quality hunts, avoid "walking and blocking" group hunts in cropland, primarily cornfields. It is a good way to get shot and it is a difficult place to control a gun dog.

6. Early season hunting often improves in late afternoon as pheasants move from cropland back into roosting cover (grasses and forbs). The closer to sunset the better. Public areas hunted hard early in the day can load up again with pheasants late in the day when most people have quit.

7. Hunt areas where the landscape has a nice mixture of cropland with grassland, wetland, and other untilled land.

8. If the landscape is almost all in cornfields or other row crops, hunt in another part of the state unless you know specific hot spots for pheasants. Row crops do not produce pheasants. Knee deep or taller grasses and forbs produce pheasants.

9. If you have a chance to hunt pheasants after the first snow, get out there immediately. In new snow, pheasants tend to hold better and gun dogs can pin the birds down for hunters.

10. Mid and late season hunting in cattails and similar heavy cover can be especially good when there is snow cover on the ground. There is usually not much competition from other hunters.

11. Even in poor pheasant years when lots of folks stay home, South Dakota always seems to have hot spots for pheasants. Just be sure to hunt after most of the crops are harvested.

12. There are almost always more pheasants than people think. Just get out and hunt and let your dog decide how many birds are out there. Don't listen too much to negative reports.

13. Get out of your vehicle and walk the cover with your gun dog. Avoid driving around all day.

14. Get away from the more heavily hunted areas on public land by walking to the back of areas.

15. Public access areas in portions of the state with high pheasant densities and high hunter densities will still have lots of pheasants even after the opening week of the general pheasant season. However, the roosters will all become track stars and you will need to outthink the birds.

16. In heavily hunted areas with no snow, push those running pheasants toward corners, roads, cattail patches or anything to encourage them to hold for a few minutes.

17. Get in good shape before hunting season by walking a few miles each day through the year with your gun dog. It could save you from a heart attack and it will make hunts more enjoyable.

Part IV. Prairie grouse—in the footsteps of pioneers

Ch. 31. Two prairie grouse species

Prairie grouse is a catch-all term used here for sharp-tailed grouse and greater prairie-chickens. Actually, South Dakota has a small population of one other sage-brush plains type grouse, the greater sage-grouse, but I do not include them here. While ring-necked pheasants get most of the attention in South Dakota and attract far more hunters than prairie grouse, the latter have their devoted followers and provide classic hunting opportunities for native game birds. Gun dogs greatly enhance hunter success and enjoyment of the hunt for prairie grouse. Sharp-tailed grouse are more broadly distributed in South Dakota than prairie chickens. Sharptails are currently found over much of the northern, central, and western portions of the state while greater prairie-chickens are much more common in some of the central and southern South Dakota counties near the Missouri River. Both of these species are native to South Dakota although sharp-tailed grouse have always been more widespread in the state; greater prairie-chickens were originally limited to the southeastern portions of the state where there was more tallgrass prairie.

Both grouse require extensive grassland habitat and have largely disappeared in southeastern South Dakota and other portions of the state where most of the native grassland has been removed. In both species, the males gather on leks (communal areas for courtship and breeding) in the spring to perform their impressive courtship dances to attract the females. Some males also gather to dance on leks in the fall. For detail on these interesting grouse including historical distributions, current distribution, population dynamics, nesting, brood rearing, and other aspects please see *Grouse of Plains and Mountains: the South Dakota Story* available through the South Dakota Department of Game, Fish and Parks.

Prairie chickens and sharp-tailed grouse are easily told apart in hand or at least up close. Prairie chickens have dark crossbars across the breast and belly and lack the elongated central tail feathers (rectrices) of sharptails. Sharptails have "V" shaped dark patterns on a white belly and breast. Most hunters new to hunting prairie grouse cannot tell the two species apart in flight but there are some good clues as you get more familiar with these remarkable birds. Sharptails have a lighter (more white) overall body coloration than the darker looking prairie chickens and generally make much more noise with their clucking on being flushed than do greater prairie-chickens.

Note the different color patterns on the breast and belly of the Greater prairie-chicken (left) and sharp-tailed grouse (right).

Both species weigh around two pounds as adults, approximately the weight of a hen pheasant. They are much better fliers than are pheasants as indicated by the darker color of the breast muscles. When flushed, both these grouse species often fly for a considerable distance. They can fly for several miles if necessary to cross the Missouri River trench or to move into new areas for wintering. Although not the norm, I have seen flocks that were making longer distance moves (primarily crossing major river trenches) that looked like they were several hundred yards above the ground.

Greater prairie-chicken over Fort Pierre National Grassland. (Courtesy of Doug Backlund)

Both sharp-tailed grouse and greater prairie-chickens are often found in small coveys or flocks in the first part of the season. They are far less able as runners than ring-necked pheasants but will occasionally amble for a few hundred yards when pushed by dogs and hunters. Both species are nicely worked by gun dogs and both hold well for pointing dogs at least from early to mid-season depending on how much they have been hunted and size of the flock. Both greater prairie-chickens and sharp-tailed grouse can be extremely difficult to approach in late season when they tend to gather in larger flocks, especially with several inches of snow covering the landscape. In mid-October in the early 1980s, Dale Gates and I flushed a large group of mostly greater prairie-chickens (probably a few sharptails) in Hand County north of Highmore that seemed to occupy an entire hillside and may have numbered over 300 birds. They flushed at least 250 yards ahead of us but a follow up on the area yielded several nice points on prairie chickens that had not flushed with the large group of birds. Seeing this many grouse together was unusual, especially that early in the season.

Hunters unfamiliar with prairie grouse sometimes have difficulty telling prairie grouse from hen pheasants or young, still drab, rooster pheasants that can also be in the same area. Sharptails can easily be separated from hen pheasants because they are so noisy with their clucking (kuk-kuk-kuk-kuk) when they take flight. The clucking of sharptails or even of the less vocal prairie chickens is a much different call than the cackling of a young cock pheasant. Sharptails also look much lighter in color than hen pheasants and the pointed tail is not nearly as long as in hen pheasants after the latter reach about 11 weeks of age. Prairie chickens have a distinctly rounded tail compared to even young pheasants.

In general, pheasants are likely to be found in heavier, taller cover than the prairie grouse but there is considerable overlap. I have flushed prairie grouse and pheasants within a few yards of each other and they are commonly in the same walk-in area, ravine, or other habitat you might be hunting in the central portions of the state closer to the Missouri River. If you are hunting for grouse and your dog trails a bird or birds for a long period of time and for a considerable distance the chances of it being a pheasant are considerable. I have trailed running pheasants while primarily hunting grouse many times but after about 200 yards of following hot scent I realize the dog is probably on the trail of a pheasant. If hunters are in extensive mixed-grass prairie landscapes in western South Dakota, they often have no problem with pheasants which tend to be nearer cropland and in heavier cover.

Male sharp-tailed grouse dancing on a lek in western South Dakota. (Courtesy of Doug Backlund)

Greater prairie-chicken dancing (booming display) on a lek on Fort Pierre National Grassland. (Courtesy of Bob Hodorff)

Ch. 32. Grouse hunting—getting started

As noted earlier, the season for prairie grouse in recent years opens the third Saturday in September and continues over three months to the end of pheasant season. Don't expect a crowd if you go hunting for prairie grouse. On the opening weekend there will be hunters on well-known areas such as the Fort Pierre National Grassland (FPNG) but, even there, you can easily find plenty of expansive grassland to work your dog. After the opening week I usually see very few grouse hunters. Hunters that prefer being alone or nearly alone with plenty of space to walk and work their hunting dog will love hunting prairie grouse.

The best method I can recommend for finding early season prairie grouse is to locate grasslands with moderate height cover, usually mixed-grass prairie, and to be ready to walk. Grassland with mixed shrubs such as chokecherry and silver buffaloberry on river break areas can also provide excellent hunting. A look at grouse survey and harvest maps in *Grouse of Plains and Mountain: The South Dakota Story* (Chapter 9 and 10) can give you a feel for areas of the state to hunt. However, please note that some western counties like Ziebach and Haakon counties show only moderate harvest levels and yet have good numbers of sharp-tailed grouse; hunters just don't care to drive that far from more urban areas in the state to hunt grouse when there are closer hunting spots.

Early in the season grouse are often feeding on grasshoppers and the leafy material or the flower parts of wild lettuce, dandelion leaves, clover, alfalfa, and other greens. If there is an abundance of prairie rose be prepared for sharptails or prairie chickens that often feed on the beautiful red fruits. They love those rose hips! The fruits on western snowberry also attract prairie grouse. Sharp-tailed grouse and greater prairie-chickens are also attracted to alfalfa fields where they feed on the leaves. In early autumn prairie grouse will opportunistically feed on grain sorghum or other crop seeds but not nearly as much as later in October and into winter. Gary Marrone, a friend and avid grouse hunter from Pierre, described the gullet contents of grouse feeding on rose hips, greens, and grasshoppers as "a colorful salad dish." Be sure to look at the crop contents as they can teach you plenty about the grouse and where to find them.

National grasslands and walk-in areas are some of the best areas to hunt prairie grouse. Private landowners will also often allow grouse hunting with permission if you don't bring a crowd. Most of my grouse hunting has been on the Fort Pierre National Grassland (FPNG), on walk-in areas, and by permission on a few private ranches. Abundance of prairie grouse in South Dakota is dependent on ample numbers of pastures with decent cover that will allow the birds to nest and rear young.

On national grasslands there is pressure to allow more cattle grazing so conditions on any national grassland can vary with the dedication and knowledge of the current Forest Service personnel in charge of management of that unit. A knowledgeable person or persons with a strong interest in keeping the grassland in good condition and in providing multiple use values for wildlife, cattle, hunters, and other allowed uses can have a strong influence on grouse habitat and grouse populations. Unfortunately, there are many examples where levels of livestock grazing have left little cover for grouse and other wildlife. In the years I have hunted the FPNG for grouse between 1990 and 2011 there have usually been many excellent pastures that held good grouse numbers. Greater prairie-chickens are generally more abundant than sharp-tailed grouse on FPNG.

Another factor to consider is severe drought. During severe drought the growth of grasses and forbs is greatly reduced and the demand for grasses for livestock forage is understandably great. Severe drought is usually accompanied by poor nesting and brood rearing success for sharptails and prairie chickens and, subsequently, poor hunting the following fall and potentially into the next year.

Ch. 33. Fort Pierre National Grassland—memorable grouse hunts

It is about a week into October in the early 2000s and Dale Gates and I drive about 30 minutes south from Pierre to hunt on the Fort Pierre National Grassland. I am visiting from Utah. Dale has had some good hunting early in the season and knows a number of areas where our chances of finding birds are good. Moisture conditions and vegetation have been favorable for a good hatch on grouse. Unlike pheasants, I do not expect to immediately be into grouse scent with my Brittany and I am prepared to walk a good number of miles looking for grouse. We eye a mile-long ridge that rises 50 to 100 feet above the surrounding plains and decide to work the main ridge plus a series of small lateral ridges. The weather will likely reach 70 degrees or better so we take water for the dogs and ourselves. There are stock ponds around but we are leery of any of these ponds that might look a bit stagnant since we had received word that a few early season grouse hunters in nearby Nebraska had lost their dogs to blue-green algae poisoning. Hunters should keep their dogs watered and look out for anything that looks like blue-green paint spilled on the water. However, scums and mats of browns and reds can also be dangerous. One rule I heard was "if its green on top, stop!

Parking on a higher ridge, the view over the national grassland is magnificent. We can see no imbedded areas of private cropland for at least a mile in any direction. The vista includes extensive mixed-grass prairie in every direction. With the troubling exception of interspersed patches of invading smooth bromegrass, the native mixed-grass prairie looks healthy and with sufficient cover to produce and hold grouse. One could walk many miles on this hunt without needing to leave these public lands. No other hunters are in sight although a camper trailer from a western state was parked closer to the highway. We have talked to the guy owning the camper trailer before—a dedicated grouse hunter who comes back to the Fort Pierre National Grassland for several weeks with his gun dogs each year.

Dale and I begin the hunt heading in the same general direction and several hundred yards apart with the dogs roaming over the prairie out to around 100 yards. When you have hunted together for over 30 years as I have with Dale Gates you know pretty much how to stay in contact but keep enough distance so that you maximize the chances of finding grouse. We watch the dogs closely for general signs that they are on hot scent and for actual points. Often you can tell the dogs have picked up hot bird scent a minute or two before they lock up on point.

After about 30 minutes of walking, the dogs get "birdy" on a secondary ridge with patches of sweetclover that are common in some years. Most of the sweetclover has dried out or been killed by an early frost but there is leafy green growth closer to the ground and grasshoppers are abundant. Prairie chickens and sharptails love grasshoppers and greens. If I tried this salad combination I would want the hoppers fried crispy. Both dogs are on fresh grouse scent and we move quickly to get closer so we are ready for the points. Dale's Brittany freezes on a beautiful point and, as Dale moves up, about 15 greater prairie-chickens burst from cover in easy range. I move toward Dale and my dog locates a single grouse close to where the flock flushed. The dark, rounded tail fan of the single prairie chicken is easily visible when it flushes so I know it is a male. The dogs quickly retrieve the two grouse we have downed.

Downed grouse are much less apt to run appreciable distances than pheasants so you are not likely to lose many grouse if you have a dog and if you watch birds closely after shooting. If a grouse acts like it is hit, try to keep the bird or flock in view as long as possible as the injured bird will often go down where it can be fetched or flushed again. It pays to carry binoculars for this purpose. Also, sometimes you can see about where a grouse flock lands and can perhaps get a second chance.

I normally use my 20-gauge Beretta and steel 4 shot on grouse. It is very effective and I often use the same combination for pheasants although size 3 steel are more lethal for pheasants.

I no longer use lead shot for bird hunting except for wild turkey loads. A lighter weight shotgun can be a real plus when you are hiking over miles of prairie looking for grouse, especially when you are in your golden years. Continuing our hunt, we run into additional prairie chickens on another lateral ridge and get two flushes of two to five birds. The dogs again get good points and we are able to move within 20 yards in each case—two more birds down.

A half hour later a coyote jumps ahead of us and quickly disappears into a draw. I like seeing a few coyotes, they kill or suppress some of the smaller predators like red fox that are more efficient at taking game birds or their eggs. Because of this phenomenon, upland game birds and upland nesting waterfowl in areas with a moderate number of coyotes tend to have better nesting success than in those areas lacking coyotes. It pays to recognize how a larger predator like a coyote can influence densities of smaller, more damaging (to nests and young) predators like the red fox. If you are interested in this topic and further literature see *Ring-necked Pheasants: Thriving in South Dakota* (pg. 101). The best answer to predation on game birds is still good grass and forb cover on the landscape. The pastures we are hunting for grouse on this day have good mixed-grass prairie cover or we would not waste time hunting them.

Less than 200 yards from where we jumped the coyote on the same ridge my dog stops on dead point and a flock of around 25 greater prairie-chickens flushes at an unusually close range. Even after years of hunting, and with the dog on point, I am startled by such a close flush of so many birds and I miss the first shot. With that covey flush and a second shot I have my three grouse limit and I'm finished hunting. We move back toward our vehicle that is now over a mile away. My dog freezes on point on some taller grass and forb cover and about nine pheasants, at least four of them cocks, flush at close range. I just watch since pheasants do not open until the third Saturday in October. On the way back Dale's dog catches strong scent and moves in to point three sharp-tailed grouse. Because of their noisy clucking, lighter overall body color, and long central tail feathers we knew they were sharptails on first flush. Dale takes a single grouse and we are now both done hunting but with a mile to hike back to the car. It has been three hours since we left the vehicle so we have put in some good mileage meandering about the prairie. We enjoyed every minute!

In most years Fort Pierre National Grassland offers good hunting for greater prairie-chickens and sharp-tailed grouse in pastures with sufficient grass and forb cover.

Following the hunt we are both convinced the grouse are concentrated on the primary and secondary ridges, especially in areas with sweetclover. The grouse gullets (crops) are loaded with grasshoppers; green, leafy vegetation from forbs; small, green shoots of grass; and the seed heads from wild lettuce. None of them have any seeds from domestic crops, a food type that will increase greatly in the diet later in the season. We get to our vehicle, gut the birds, put them on ice in a cooler (hot day), and drive the unpaved dirt road back toward the highway. If it is rainy these roads can get plenty messy because of the clay soils but fortunately the roads are dry.

The grouse hunter and a fellow hunter are at the camper we saw earlier and we stop to exchange stories. We find out that they similarly had great luck just a couple of miles northwest of where we hunted but had found the grouse in the lowlands. Our theory that they were on the ridges crashes. What was the similarity? Their grouse were loaded with grasshoppers and dandelion leaves so, like ours, they were in spots where both grasshoppers and greens were abundant. Since grasshoppers were plentiful almost everywhere on the grassland that year, we decide appropriate greens were the diet item most affecting grouse location.

When you hunt grouse be ready to hike and enjoy the scenery and the wildlife. Meadowlarks, short-eared owls, northern harriers, coyotes, and more, it is all fun to see. Keep walking and working and you will usually find a few flocks of grouse. When you get grouse in hand, note what they are eating and look at the area where you found them. That will make it easier to find grouse the next time. Most grouse hunters will have some success but those that look at the diet and keep a written or mental record of where they find grouse are usually more successful than others who pay little attention to such matters.

We end the hunt with five prairie chickens and one sharp-tailed grouse and that ratio is not a surprise on the FPNG where greater prairie-chickens tend to be more abundant than sharptails. We head back to Pierre with plans to be back on the grasslands hunting grouse the next morning.

The next morning I am back hunting alone in the same area and feeling sorry for Dale because he had to cancel vacation time due to urgent matters at work. Within 200 yards of the vehicle my dog is on point on a covey of greater prairie-chickens. I get close before they flush and I can easily see their color patterns. I walk another half hour and the dog is on point again. Nice flock of prairie chickens. Twenty minutes later she is on point again on a small flock of sharp-tailed grouse. I'm surprised to finish in little over an hour. It is unusual to get into so many grouse so quickly but this day the hunt is over. I finish out the morning catching bluegills on my fly rod on one of the many stock ponds on the FPNG.

The next morning Dale joins me and we hunt again on the FPNG at another good looking spot and probably walk over 10 miles with grouse much harder to find and seemingly more wary that day. We flush a flock of over 30 grouse, mostly prairie chickens, but they flush wild and out of range. We eventually get a few points and end up with two birds apiece. Two of the grouse are sharptails, two are prairie chickens. In a couple of spots along an intermittent stream we flush several pheasants but the season is closed. At one point I hear the chirping of prairie dogs before I see the mounds and the residents. I avoid the small dog town to lower the chances of my dog encountering a prairie rattlesnake. We have hunted hard for about five hours. Still, long day or short day I love to grouse hunt on the prairies. So much wildlife and a feeling like it could be the 1800s again.

Dale Gate's Brittany (BJ) is pointing a small covey of greater prairie-chickens about 20 feet in front of the dog on this picturesque ridge on Fort Pierre National Grassland (2008).

Ch. 34. Sorry, I've already promised the area to friends

In late September in the 1990s Jon Jenks and I traveled to the Little Moreau Game Refuge to attend a game staff research meeting held by the South Dakota Department of Game, Fish and Parks (SDGFP). Jon was a fellow faculty member in the Wildlife and Fisheries Sciences Department at SDSU and a close friend. We headed to this West River site in northern South Dakota a couple of days early so we could hunt sharptails and gray partridge on the weekend before the meetings. We located a large ranch that a friend had recommended on the breaks of the Moreau River or one of its tributaries. The ranch and the river breaks looked like beautiful sharp-tailed grouse habitat and we found the rancher and his wife at home. The rancher (Pete) was over 80 years old and very cordial but told us he had already reserved the grouse hunting for the season and did not want additional hunters. He did however telephone his son and sent us to hunt grouse on that land which was only a few miles away. It turned out to be a good area for grouse and gray partridge.

Late in the afternoon we noted a vehicle driving slowly along a dirt road, parallel to where we were hunting. We assumed the two people in the vehicle were watching us hunt. Concerned that we might have gotten on the wrong land, we walked the few hundred yards over to the vehicle; it turned out to be the older rancher we had talked to earlier in the day along with his wife. He told us to be at his place at 7 a.m. the next morning to hunt grouse. I think we had been put through a preliminary test to see how we hunted. He apparently appreciated hunters that got out of the vehicle and walked instead of trying to drive around pastures looking for grouse. We passed the test and after that we were welcome on his ranch. We hunted that river break ranch with excellent success for the next several years. When Pete died, we were surprised to learn that he had left word with his son to let the two guys from Brookings hunt grouse.

Ch. 35. You can hunt grouse but my ranch is pretty small

Tim Modde is a long-time friend and fisheries biologist that was a fellow faculty member at SDSU for several years before taking another position elsewhere. We keep in contact and, in fact, went bow hunting for elk in Utah's Uintah Mountains a few years ago and had the memorable experience of accidentally calling a mountain lion to within 30 yards using our cow elk calls. The lion and hunters were all most surprised!

In the 1970s, Tim and I were in Gregory County in late September or early October near the Missouri River and had stopped at a ranch to ask the rancher if we could hunt sharp-tailed grouse along some river break country near his ranch house. The steep breaks looked like perfect sharp-tailed grouse habitat along with some possibility of greater prairie-chickens in the area. The rancher and Tim had both attended the University of South Dakota at the same time and the rancher remembered that Tim, a defensive end on the football team, had intercepted the football and scored a touchdown against SDSU. The rancher told us we could hunt on his land but that he did not have a very large ranch. He then proceeded to tell us that his ranch included all of the land we had asked about, an area that included a mile-wide strip of land south of the highway out to a full four miles west of the ranch house, at least four square miles. Four square miles seemed like a lot of land to us and I'm sure that was not the extent of his or his families land.

In the ensuing hunt the dogs found hundreds of sharp-tailed grouse, many concentrated at the top of the river breaks in a field of knee-high grain sorghum that the rancher told us we could hunt. Don't be surprised if the ranch you get permission on covers thousands of acres. Ranchers and ranchlands protect much of the remaining native grassland and are critical to the future of prairie grouse and many other prairie-dependent animals and plants. The ranchers and their families are also some pretty nice folks.

Private ranchland and sharp-tailed grouse country along the Bad River in western South Dakota.

Ranchers and ranchlands offer the best hope for the future of sharp-tailed grouse and greater-prairie chicken populations in South Dakota.

Ch. 36. Badlands, sharptails, and rattlesnakes

It was late October in 2008 and Gary Peterson and I had travelled to South Dakota from Utah to hunt grouse and pheasants. Gary was on the faculty at SDSU in the Biology Department during the entire time I was at that university and we often hunted and fished together. He and his wife Pam were like family to us with our children growing up together. Gary's wife died of cancer a few years ago and he moved back to northern Utah to be closer to where Pam is buried. We still fish together and have had some great times catching salmon on fly rods in Alaska and trying to stay out of the way of brown bears that want the same fishing hole.

Gary and I were hunting sharp-tailed grouse with my Brittany and Gary's Labrador retriever on a walk-in area that covered over 6,000 acres a few miles east of Badlands National Park. Our approach, as in most sharp-tailed grouse hunts, was to start hiking across the landscape, working grasslands, shrubs along drainages, moist bottomlands, and other likely spots. The only other hunters we saw on this expansive area were two guys bow hunting for mule deer. And yes, we saw our share of mule deer in the draws and ravines during the hunt. It was difficult to pinpoint areas that were more likely to hold grouse but the best spots proved to be moist ravines, brushy hillsides near stock ponds, and a grassland flat adjacent to a private alfalfa field.

We were having good success but we had to walk several miles to find the scattered coveys and flocks of sharptails. The largest flock of grouse we put up had over 30 birds. As we were returning to our vehicle after one outing, a rancher approached us on his four-wheeler (ATV). He had two farm dogs running alongside and he wanted to visit about his success finding rattlesnakes. He had killed five rattlers that morning at prairie dog towns where the snakes commonly start gathering before winter denning time. Prairie rattlesnakes are also fairly common near the dog towns during the summer and earlier in the fall. His two dogs were apparently well trained at finding rattlers in these prairie dog towns and they knew how to avoid getting bitten. While hunting that day we had encountered a couple of prairie dog towns and had circled around to avoid these areas to protect our hunting dogs. You can usually see the mounds around dens or, even earlier, hear the chirping of the prairie dogs. After seeing those dead rattlesnakes, most of them close to 25-30 inches, we were even more concerned about the dogs running into rattlers. The largest rattlesnake looked to be about 40 inches in length and of considerable girth.

A few hours later as we were leaving in our vehicle we saw the same rancher driving his ATV toward the roadside and motioning to us. We stopped and he proudly held up his sixth rattler, a three-foot beauty that he had just bagged. I'm always impressed by ranchers who are so close to the land and who provide so much important habitat. His ranch was huge and it was well managed in terms of grassland condition. So many wildlife species and native plants benefit from such ranches. The last memory I have of that spot was a golden eagle soaring in front of my jeep patriot as we drove along the edge of the ranch. The ranch was still signed up in the walk-in program the last I checked in fall of 2013.

Prairie rattlesnakes are more likely to be encountered around prairie dog towns. (Courtesy of Doug Backlund)

Ch. 37. An Intermittent stream and grouse

I had hunted a west-river walk-in area in northern South Dakota for two hours that November (about 2011) morning and had flushed a couple of skittish coveys of sharptails at over 70 yards. My dog, Brook, had also pointed a nice flock of over a dozen gray partridge less than 10 feet from me in a single-row shelterbelt but the trees and partridge won that round without me even firing a shot. I especially like to get a few partridge since they taste great and the feathers are valuable in tying a couple of my favorite trout nymphs. Try to purchase a partridge skin (about $25) at a fly tying store and you can see why I borax the skins and keep the feathers.

After meeting up with two of my friends from Idaho, Jack Connelly and Doug Finicle, and eating lunch together, I left them to hunt their favorite spot and drove about a mile to a popular walk-in area that was being hunted by a couple of groups earlier in the day. Jack and Doug had well trained German shorthairs and Brittanys and had scored on a couple of grouse and pheasants before lunch. They knew where to look for me if I got in trouble and hunting a separate area gave everyone more space. Fortunately, the two other groups that were hunting the area had moved on to new grounds. I'm pretty sure they did not walk as far back from the road as I had planned.

The walk-in area covered almost two square miles and included an intermittent stream, extensive lowland areas (dry wetlands) dominated by dock weed, and uplands dominated by mixed-grass prairie and invading smooth brome. Portions of the dry wetland areas dominated by dock weed were easily identified by the reddish, dark color of the leaves and mature seed heads. Problem areas to avoid were cactus flats that were intimidating to my Brittany and kept me busy pulling cactus with my pliers. The area was bordered on the north side by harvested fields of corn and sunflowers. Cropland made up less than 30% of the landscape.

Because of the earlier hunting pressure from pheasant hunters near the road I headed across the uplands and along the edge of a large dry wetland flat to reach the intermittent stream. The stream section was almost a half mile from the road, enough distance to discourage many of the hunters primarily after pheasants. On my way to the stream Brook and I had a small flock of sharp-tailed grouse flush wild from a hillside, at least one out of range flush of a running rooster, and a couple of points on hen pheasants. These hunts are never dull!

The meandering streambed featured a combination of mixed grasses on the adjacent uplands and denser, taller vegetation along the edge of the stream. Pools of water occurred periodically and there were linear cattail patches here and there. The stream quarters away from the road and, fortunately for me, looks like nothing special for hunting when viewed from cover closer to road. At least not special enough to bother walking very far. From earlier hunts, I knew better.

The first memorable action along the streambed occurred when I bumped an enormous 6 x 6 white-tailed buck from a cattail patch along the stream. At 15 feet his antlers looked wide and beautiful and the broad back jiggled with fat as he thundered off along the drainage way. I love these encounters with wildlife! A few years ago I walked up to a dry creek bed in a native prairie landscape and found myself within 10 feet of a golden eagle that was sunning itself along the creek bank. Both of us were surprised! The variety of wildlife hunters encounter in native prairie and wetland areas in South Dakota makes for especially interesting days.

Within 200 yards from where I jumped the buck, Brook pinned down a covey of sharptails on a narrow grassy peninsula between meanders of the streambed. A half dozen sharptails were holding on that site and flushed in somewhat staggered fashion at close range. Like sharptails usually do, they made plenty of cackling (kuk, kuk, kuk) as they flushed and flew off. Pretty noisy birds when they flush near you. I shot and missed but recovered to down a single grouse with my 20-gauge Berretta. About three minutes later, within 30 feet of where the grouse flushed, the dog pointed a rooster pheasant in a patch of denser and taller grass. I swung on the rooster and Brook made the retrieve. Within an hour Brook pointed two other coveys of sharp-tailed grouse at close range along the intermittent stream plus another single rooster at my feet.

We were about 1.5 miles from the vehicle by the time I shot my last grouse and I was confident that Brook would find that last rooster pheasant on the way back to the vehicle. Keys to this being a hidden grouse jewel were distance from road access and the nice mixture of habitats including dry wetlands dominated by dock weed, the meandering creek bed with its variable vegetation, and the cowboy boot-high mixed-grass prairie on the flats and small hills. The nearby cropland becomes increasingly important to prairie grouse in mid to late season when grasshoppers and green, leafy vegetation become scarce. Of course, as on most upland bird hunts, I would have found far fewer birds without a gun dog.

As for the pheasant bonus, I have always been a bit surprised by how many pheasants I found on this area but I am sure the nearby cropland had a big effect plus some of the denser areas of cover were important. There always seem to be several roosters hanging along the heavier cover associated with the creek bed, especially where it meanders farthest from the road. Those rooster pheasants know how to get away from the crowds. I'm also confident that a moderate population of coyotes to control smaller predators like red fox (more specialized at finding nests) has an overall positive influence on the pheasant and grouse populations in this area.

Ch. 38. Prairie grouse and Russian olives

Russian olives are exotic trees that can spread and cause problems in the plains states. Nevertheless, they have been widely introduced in shelterbelts and around farmsteads due to their drought tolerance. In prairie regions of western and central South Dakota sharp-tailed grouse are often attracted to tree belts with Russian olives because of the fruit and, on hot days, their shade.

Jack Connelly and I were hunting a Game Production Area (GPA) in western South Dakota for sharp-tailed grouse and pheasants. We were camped at a small reservoir with public camping sites immediately adjacent to the GPA. Early in the morning when we could hunt only grouse (pheasant shooting hours open at 9 a.m.), Jack had headed for his favorite area on this large Game Production Area (GPA). From our campsite, I had watched several flocks of sharp-tailed grouse flying from some distance across the small reservoir and landing in a series of dense but narrow shelterbelts with junipers and Russian Olive. Some birds even landed in a tall adjacent dead cottonwood before gliding down into the junipers and Russian olives. The flight of flocks of sharptails into these tree belts was impressive but did not last long enough for me to get set up for some pass shooting. I assumed the Russian olive fruit was the primary attraction although juniper berries are sometimes eaten in winter.

Without Jack and one of his German shorthairs to walk the opposite side of these dense tree belts, I tried to hunt alone. Bad idea! There were plenty of grouse in those trees. In fact, in less than five acres of intermixed shelterbelts and grass I must have flushed over 100 sharp-tailed grouse that were feeding in the trees. I would get close to the birds and the dog would be on point but the feeding grouse invariably flushed out the other side of the tree belts giving me no good shots and a few tough ones. The single grouse I downed had Russian olive fruit in its gullet.

Oh yes, Jack ran into fewer but more vulnerable grouse in the more open habitat of grass, weeds, and shrubs (snowberry) that he hunted.

On another West River ranch with healthy grouse numbers I had often hunted the grassland cover with good success but I also knew that a twin-row tree belt of mid age Russian olive always had grouse if I was having trouble finding them elsewhere. The trees looked healthy and each year seemed loaded with fruit. In hunting those trees I had learned my lesson and almost always tried to have one person on each side of the tree belt as we worked our dog or dogs through those Russian olives. You could bank on finding grouse either feeding or loafing in this belt of Russian olive trees. The other parts of the ranch were also excellent with native grasses and grouse throughout. Every time I hunted this great ranch I flushed multiple coveys of sharptails. Great grouse hunting and wonderful prairie habitat!

Unfortunately, virtually all the sharp-tailed grouse habitat on this area (over 2,000 acres) was recently plowed and turned into a huge sunflower field when a large corporation purchased this land. Bad for the grouse, bad for other wildlife, bad for the native grassland plants, and a great way to lose the marginal soils on the area to wind and water. Continued loss of native grasslands, particularly on marginal soil areas, is an incredible tragedy for South Dakota.

Ch. 39. Shrubs and more shrubs

It was toward midday in late September and the temperatures were a little over 70 degrees Fahrenheit with almost no wind. I was hunting alone in river break country in western South Dakota. I knew the sharptails were probably loafing in a cool spot so I started pushing brushy draws where the birds might be holding in the shade. As I approached a patch of silver buffaloberry my Brittany slowed and then locked on point. The space around me erupted with wings and distressed calls of sharp-tailed grouse (kuk-kuk-kuk-kuk) as over 15 birds took to the air. If it is hot, be sure to work shrub patches in draws, ravines, or other areas. They can be productive for sharptails.

In another situation on a late afternoon hunt I was pushing grassland draws and slopes in the Little Moreau Recreation Area in northern South Dakota. I had hunted less than a half hour when I worked the dog toward a snowberry patch that covered at least a half-acre of land. The snowberry patch was loaded with sharptails and I would guess over 50 grouse filled the air on my approach, all of them jumping out of effective gun range. About 150 yards away from where the original flock jumped my dog pointed a single on which I made a poor shot. The grouse flew back toward the snowberry patch where the large flock had flushed and appeared to go down in that brushy cover. I hate losing a bird and I searched for that bird for at least 30 minutes before my dog pointed and captured it. While searching for the original bird I flushed three or four sharptails at close range that had remained in the large snowberry patch when the original flock flushed. Each bird held on point and flushed within five yards of me. On sharptails and prairie chickens in early to mid-season, be prepared for those late holding birds after the main flock has flown. I have learned to give my dog a chance to further work the scent on these areas and it has been a good strategy.

On your grouse hunts, be sure to work those brushy patches that may provide food, shade, or protection (from aerial predators).

Ch. 40. Peering prairie grouse—it's about vegetation height

It was early October in northcentral South Dakota and I was hunting sharp-tailed grouse on a walk-in area that covered almost a square mile. About a fourth of the walk-in area had been seeded into intermediate wheatgrass so it was fairly tall (about 30 inches) and dense. At the time I had not hunted sharptails very often and was still developing my image of where to best find these birds. I knew the general area had plenty of sharptails. The intermediate wheatgrass turned out to be good pheasant cover and the dog and I watched as several roosters held nicely on point, flushing in easy range. However, it was not pheasant season and I was not finding sharp-tailed grouse.

After about an hour of flushing pheasants, I began avoiding the taller cover of seeded intermediate wheatgrass and moved onto areas dominated by native mixed-grass prairie. These native grass areas covered knolls, ridges, and lowlands and had a diversity of low to intermediate height grasses and forbs mixed in with pockets of snowberry and some wild rose. It was not long before my Brittany slowed and locked on point. Directly upwind, within 10 yards, a covey of sharptails in easy range of my 20 gauge made plenty of clucking to announce their departure. My dog retrieved a single sharptail and I admired the beautiful white and dark (v marks) colors on the breast and belly. The two elongated central tail feathers of this male sharptail had longitudinal patterns of dark and light colors compared to the more cross-barred pattern on the females. The more pointed and narrow outer two primaries (flight feathers) and the half-inch deep bursal measurement in the rectum told me it was a juvenile (see Chapter 2: *Grouse of Plains and Mountains: The South Dakota Story*). The remainder of this hunt was productively spent locating additional sharptails on these intermediate height native grasslands. It was a most rewarding day and I learned to mostly avoid large expanses of tall, dense grass when hunting sharp-tailed grouse.

It is not uncommon to be hunting sharptails or greater prairie-chickens and look ahead to see one or two birds, necks stretched out, and peering at you from the intermediate height cover. They may even put a sentry bird or two on a high point or, occasionally, even in a tree. In my opinion, sharptails like to be able to see around themselves as a defense against predators. Even greater prairie-chickens, a bird specialized for tallgrass prairies, seem to like disturbed openings in tallgrass prairie areas that are dominated by shorter vegetation and greens important for food. Greater prairie-chickens were native to southeastern portions of South Dakota that were dominated by tallgrass prairie. However, with the availability of waste grains in winter, they have apparently adapted quite well to areas on the edge or outside of their original range in portions of central and south central South Dakota that are dominated mainly by mixed-grass prairie.

In the mid-1990s I was hunting in western South Dakota on a walk-in area with grass that was taller than I would normally pick for hunting sharp-tailed grouse. The grasses were tall enough that they would make it difficult for the grouse to see for any distance. However, earlier I had watched two flocks of sharptails fly into this area as I drove along the highway. Walking into the area, I found numerous small openings (most less than a quarter of an acre) with dandelions, wild lettuce, several other forbs, and shorter grasses. This turned out to be one of my favorite grouse spots in western South Dakota. The dog found plenty of grouse in or close to these embedded openings and we had some great hunts on this spot. So, dense grass up to your thighs or waist is usually not so good for sharp-tailed grouse hunts in South Dakota, but moderately tall or tallgrass with numerous embedded openings containing grouse food plants and shorter cover can be very good. Volunteer sweetclover can be tall but it is patchy and has food value so it can be good cover for prairie grouse.

Ch. 41. Prairie grouse know it's warmer on the lee side

I was hunting sharptails on an extensive walk-in area with plenty of hills and ridges South of Belvidere in late October. Temperatures were relatively cool for late October and there was a brisk afternoon wind. I had hiked in almost a mile, crossing a wide and deep ravine and climbing a few hundred feet back onto a ridge on the opposite side. I had not seen a grouse in almost an hour of hiking although the dog and I did find a porcupine and jumped a beautiful mule deer buck. Fortunately, my dog stayed a few feet away from the porcupine. We had a farm dog get into a porcupine when I was a kid in central Oregon and it was not a fun day. As I hiked up the far ridge I found an abundance of wild rose (rose hips) and snowberry mixed with grasses and forbs and the whole scenario made me pay close attention, feeling like grouse should be close. Harvested corn and sorghum were also within a mile, easy flying distance for grouse. I primarily hunted the leeward side of the ridge as I pushed forward. Experience had taught me that grouse would use the lee side of the ridge more than the windy side in an effort to get out of the cool or cold wind.

As I moved along the lee side of the ridge line the dog caught grouse scent and moved forward slowly. I saw a few grouse heads pop up, looking for an approaching predator. At that moment over a dozen grouse flushed about 25 yards ahead, caught the wind, and left me with nothing but a spent shell. Fortunately, the lee side of that ridge was loaded with more grouse and provided some beautiful points by my Brittany. Brook must have found at least 50 grouse along that ridge, some as singles or small groups that thought they could hunker down until the danger was over. I started the long hike back to my vehicle with three sharp-tailed grouse and more evidence that grouse seek comfortable (out of the cool or cold wind), secluded spots, with the right kind of food and cover. If you are in good prairie grouse habitat in an area with ravines or ridges, hunting the lee side when the wind is cool or cold can increase your chances of finding grouse. Just ask yourself, where would the grouse be most comfortable under the existing conditions?

On cool or cold, windy days, look for sharp-tailed grouse on the protected lee side of hills and draws. This is the Lower White River Game Production Area.

Ch. 42. A long trip home but time for one quick hunt

It was the second week in November in 2012 and I had been hunting pheasants and grouse in South Dakota (as a nonresident) for over two weeks. As per usual, I was on my second 10-day license for upland game. The weather indicated I had better get moving on the approximately 15-hour drive to Springville, Utah, if I wanted to beat a major snowstorm destined to hit Wyoming. I was staying with Dale and Natalie Gates in Pierre and Dale kept telling me I needed to stop for a couple of hours to hunt sharp-tailed grouse on a walk-in area hot spot along Highway 14. I headed west and about 90 minutes later stopped to look at the spot Dale had recommended. The walk-in area stretched for a full mile away from the road but the first half mile from the road was mowed and had no grouse cover. It looked like decent grass cover in the back portions with a harvested wheat field along the distant edge. The back portion looked like it had good potential for sharptails and I surmised that few hunters would waste time with the long walk across the half mile of mowed area closest to the road.

Looking at my watch, I thought of the long drive ahead, the oncoming snowstorm, and my penchant to just keep hunting once I start. Again ignoring all common sense, I walked the half mile of mowed and harvested grass and found the back half of the section covered with knee-high grass along with intermixed alfalfa and sweetclover. Much of the vegetation had already lost the green coloration due to heavy frost. This type of mixed grass-forb cover can be especially attractive to prairie grouse and pheasants. I worked the dog for less than 45 minutes in this great cover, getting points on three flocks of sharp-tailed grouse and a couple of singles—no pheasants. One flock had over 30 birds with the other two having less than 10. Most of the grouse were within a quarter mile of the harvested wheat field. The points by my Brittany, the flushing grouse, the noisy clucking of the sharptails, and the dog retrieves would provide great memories on the way home and even now. What a remarkable hunt in such a short time. I gutted the grouse near an intermittent stream and headed back to my jeep. Within two hours after leaving the vehicle, I was back at the car ready to head west. Thanks for the tip Dale!

As for the snowstorm, I hit heavy snow and slushy road conditions an hour east of Evanston Wyoming and drove the rest of the way home more than a little concerned about a high-speed collision or ending up in the ditch as had several other cars and a truck along the way. Still, I'll be remembering this trip and the last-minute grouse hunt for the rest of my life. These kinds of memories linger in your mind and bring you back for more South Dakota hunting in future years.

Just one last grouse hunt, one last point on my way back to Utah. Brook on point on a large covey of sharp-tailed grouse in early November 2012.

Ch. 43. A list of suggestions to improve your success hunting prairie grouse

Gary Marrone was the state fisheries biologist in South Dakota for many years before retirement. He is the most dedicated sharp-tailed grouse and greater prairie-chicken hunter that I know. Since retirement, Gary hunts prairie grouse around Pierre with his Gordon setter in the fall before heading down to the gulf coast for a winter of fishing for redfish and other ocean fish with his wife Sally. I keep tabs on them because Gary is conscientious about sending his friends tormenting photos of 30-pound redfish, and other enviable catches from their wintering location on the Texas gulf coast. Gary suggested I add the list of suggestions for grouse hunters (and pheasant hunters) and helped me with ideas on the grouse list. Hunters new to hunting prairie grouse or hunters just wanting to improve their success may want to look this over.

The prairie grouse list:

1. A hunting dog will definitely improve your chances for finding and retrieving grouse.

2. If you are hunting ridges, walk on the lee side on cool windy days. If you hunt ridges with broad slopes, the areas near the top of the ridge seem to be prime spots.

3. Lowland areas can be excellent if they have an abundance of greens and grasshoppers.

4. Look for areas of mixed grasses and forbs. Plants like wild lettuce and dandelions are favorite greens for prairie grouse. Sweetclover, alive or residual, is attractive to prairie grouse.

5. Avoid expansive areas of seeded intermediate wheatgrass, crested wheatgrass, or even invasive smooth brome, especially if they contain few forbs and few embedded open areas.

6. Generally avoid areas of tall, dense grass that lack embedded openings unless you are hunting both grouse and pheasants. Even though greater prairie-chickens evolved in tallgrass prairies, they still seem to like the disturbed spots with

Finding Paradise in South Dakota

shorter vegetation and openings where they are better able to see around them.

7. Avoid areas that look like they have been grazed hard by cattle or sheep. Gary Marrone suggests a minimum of at least one foot of concealing vegetation. Dale Gates and I have sometimes found good grouse numbers in vegetation providing about 10 inches of concealment if the grasshopper and forb components were good.

8. A mosaic of shrubs mixed in with native grasses and forbs plus an abundance of grasshoppers are all good signs. Sharptails and greater prairie-chickens are often associated with wild rose (rose hips) and snowberry patches.

9. Wild plum and silver buffaloberry thickets can all be hot spots. On hot days grouse may be resting and loafing in the shade of these large shrubs.

10. Nearby water is a positive but is not usually necessary. Early season grouse get needed water from green vegetation, berries, and grasshoppers.

11. Having waste grain (corn, sunflowers, sorghum) in close proximity is good but not necessary early in the season. As the season progresses and grasshoppers and green vegetation become less available, grouse will likely be closer to fields with waste grain.

12. Short grain sorghum is irresistible to prairie grouse even early in the fall.

13. Periodically flooded wetland areas (usually flooded in the spring) dominated by dock weed often include small forbs and are attractive to prairie grouse. These areas also often have small embedded open areas where grouse like to sit.

14. Intermittent streams with abundant forbs, grasses, and shrub patches can be hot spots. If the uplands are unusually dry, the green vegetation in draws and ravines or along intermittent streams can be especially attractive for grouse.

15. Try to approach thickets of wild plum and other likely looking spots from downwind. Your gun dog will usually give you early warning of birds ahead.

16. Cover lots of territory, working the most likely patches of attractive habitat. If you are with another person, spread out

on the landscape. If you have a pointing dog, let the dog cover lots of territory to increase the numbers of grouse you will find.

17. Watch for clusters of grouse droppings as evidence of roosting areas. Returning to these areas late in the day can pay dividends.

18. If you run into a windbreak containing Russian olive trees, be aware that sharp-tailed grouse are attracted by the abundant fruit produced by these trees and also use the trees for shade (loafing) on hot days.

19. Be watchful for rattlesnakes and especially avoid black-tailed prairie dog towns where they often congregate.

20. If the grouse are feeding in adjacent cropland, watch for flocks of returning grouse flying back into the grassland you are hunting. You can often see them land and then plan your approach.

21. If you flush a flock of grouse there may still be a straggler or two hiding tight in the cover. It can pay to give the dog a chance to go over the spot again.

If you have a pointing dog, let the dog cover lots of territory when hunting sharptails and prairie chickens. Here, Brook shows interest in fresh grouse scent so I should move in closer.

Part V. Gun dogs—keys to great hunts

Ch. 44. Getting started with your own hunting dog

Dogs such as Llewellyn setters, German short hairs, Labrador retrievers, golden retrievers, wire-haired pointers, springer spaniels, Gordon setters, Brittanys, and several others can make good upland bird dogs and family pets. For me it was a priority that my gun dogs also be good family pets. It is not necessary to try and get the most expensive, best field trial dog you can find. Sometimes wide ranging, rapid moving, award winning field trial genetics is not what you really need. I'm not against purchasing dogs from award winning lines, I'm just not sure it is worth a lot of extra money unless you plan to breed the dog and sell the puppies for a substantial sum. In purchasing a hunting dog, I'm primarily interested in the hunting abilities and social behavior (around people and other dogs) of the parents and the pup.

If you purchase a hunting dog you need to be prepared to take it out walking or otherwise let it run on a daily or every other day basis; that should help keep you in good health as well. I chose a Brittany because a couple of friends had Brittanys and because I thought it would make a good family pet as well as hunting dog. Including a new pup (Dakota) brought home in October 2014, I have owned five Brittanys since my first in 1972, all females. In each case, we brought the puppy home by seven weeks of age so she could be properly adopted by our family. We house trained each puppy by keeping her in a small containment area or dog kennel in our house except when we took her outside or were watching her closely. The puppies generally avoided soiling the inside of the portable dog kennel or small play area if we would take them out periodically and let them run around on the lawn. In this manner they soon learned that the place to relieve themselves was in the yard, not in the house. We also taught each of our hunting dogs to stay off of the carpets, a lesson they learned quickly. Most dog ownership books provide ideas on how to house train puppies.

Hunting dogs get very attached to families and especially to the person who hunts them. In reverse, the family often gets attached to the hunting dog and that makes everything better, especially if your spouse and children like the dog. If your spouse does not care for the dog, don't be worried as that is not too uncommon. In that case, I recommend keeping the spouse and, if necessary, moving the dog to the outdoor kennel and fenced yard. Marcia liked all of our Brittanys but was least fond of two of our Brittanys that continually got into trouble in the house—they found themselves living in the outside kennel except for regular in-house visits.

Kim, Margo, and Ryan (from left to right) with our puppy Rascal in Brookings (1984).

You can spend the dollars for professional gun dog training but I trained my own dogs and I learned along with the dogs. You first need to teach the dog a few basic commands like heel, stay, come, no, whoa (I use "back" since no sounds like whoa), and fetch. Dog training books provide ideas on training methods but most of these commands are easily taught at home or in the field with regular repetition. For example, on daily hikes I would make my dog "stay" until I hiked ahead out of sight and yelled "come." I also use the hiking opportunities to have dogs practice staying at heel. One of my hunting companions, Jack Connelly, told me he starts training hunting dogs at 10 weeks but limits the training sessions to around 10 minutes per day. He also recommends ending training sessions on a positive note. These are both good suggestions.

To help pups develop as hunting dogs, the primary approach I took was to get the dog close to as many wild pheasants (or other upland game birds) as possible. It can greatly help in getting a new pup ready if you take the pup on pretend hunts during late afternoons in August and September prior to the grouse and pheasant seasons. If you know where pheasants, sharp-tailed grouse, or other game birds are gathering to loaf or roost for the night, such areas can make good places to train your pup. Getting that first point on a wild pheasant prior to the hunting season was always a gratifying and promising experience with my Brittany pups. I distinctly remember taking my approximately five month old pup (Kali) down a fenceline where I had watched a rooster pheasant run into the grass cover. The wind was blowing our direction and the pup and I walked along the fenceline until this pup reached the point where the pheasant had been and froze on a beautiful point near the hidden rooster. She might have sight pointed a few robins or grasshoppers before that but this was the first live game bird. What a thrill that first solid point brings to the trainer! Things will only get better and better after that first point on a game bird, especially if you hunt the dog on a frequent basis. Be aware of state laws on the legality of running hunting dogs on private and public lands. For example, in South Dakota it is illegal to train gun dogs on wild birds from April 15 through July 31.

I have started seriously hunting pups on pheasants or prairie grouse as young as 6 months. For two of the five Brittanys that I trained and hunted with (four of my own and a friends pup), the first point on a live game bird was on the first day of their first pheasant or grouse hunt. In my experience, my Brittanys developed their hunting and pointing abilities by hunting the dog plenty of hours on a regular basis. Shooting the first bird over your dog and having her help find the bird confirms that you definitely have a hunting dog and hunting companion. There are other excellent training methods like setting out pigeons or pen reared quail but I have not used this approach. Living in South Dakota, it was just too easy to take the dog in the field and find wild birds. Fortunately, my Brittanys all pointed quite naturally and right away when they got close to pheasants or grouse.

Until I have fired the shotgun around a puppy I have some concern that it might be gun shy. One of my pups, Brook, seemed frightened by loud noises such as clanging pans together or even hitting nails with a hammer. Of course, I was concerned about her possible reaction to a shotgun. At the time, I was framing the basement on our new home and needed to shoot cement nails into the base 2 x 4 of each frame. The loud bang from the cement nail gun pushed my fearful puppy to the far end of the basement or upstairs. She loved to play chase so I decided to try and make each "bang" of the 22-caliber nail gun part of a game. I would put her at the far end of the basement, make her stay, and then go to the other end and set another cement nail in a frame. With each loud bang I would run around the entire basement and Brook would respond by chasing me. When she caught me I would pet her and then would put her back on the other end of the basement and do the same thing again. She was soon anticipating the loud bang and came running to me as soon as she heard the bang. She loved the game and I had no problems with her becoming gun shy.

With the other dogs I had similarly used clanging pots and pans or the firing of a 22-caliber rifle accompanied by chasing and playing. I also would take a friend and the puppy into the field and while one person was shooting at clay pigeons at a distance from the dog, the other would play chase with the puppy, moving closer and closer to the shooting. Soon the dog would be taking no particular notice when the shotgun was fired.

Of course, as the dog learns to hunt, the sight or sound of a shotgun becomes a positive experience for them and they get fired up to go hunting if you even pick up a firearm. In most cases I was hunting each puppy by six to 10 months, depending on when the pup was born.

Discussing hunting dogs reminds me of a student in a college class I was teaching at South Dakota State University (SDSU). Some of the junior and senior students as well as graduate students at SDSU had hunting dogs of their own. A junior student came to my ornithology class one day with bandages across his nose and above his mouth. He looked like he had been in a pretty bad accident and probably had some stitches. The other students told me that he had come home drunk one night and decided to tease his roommates hunting dog by getting down on his hands and knees and pretending like he was going to eat the dog's food pellets. The dog naturally protected his food! Sorry about the injury but I figured this guy earned that one.

Ch. 45. Training to retrieve

Bird hunters will want to train their dog to retrieve birds. Dog training books present different methods for teaching gun dogs to retrieve including forced retrieving methods and more voluntary methods that keep things fun for you and the dog. The retrieving instinct often seems natural but training is still needed. I usually have trained my dogs to retrieve by using a balled up pair of socks and tossing them into a small room (such as a bathroom) where the dog needs to come back by me after naturally picking up the tossed socks. By repeatedly saying "fetch" and then "give" and taking the socks back from the dog, they will usually get the idea. Then I move outside and start using a wing from a pheasant or duck to practice.

In the first year I never push the dog on actual retrieves of crippled pheasants because of concern they could get spurred. Still, some of my pups have insisted on fetching running pheasants even in the first year. It might be best to start initial retrieves on birds like sharp-tailed grouse or gray partridge, birds that are not going to spur the pup.

In spring 1973, when we brought home our first Brittany, Pepsi, we lived on the edge of town (Brookings) with an alfalfa field behind our yard. This Indian Hills development is now all housing. I would practice with my dog by having her "sit and stay" in the front yard while I went around the house and out into the alfalfa field and flung the pheasant wing into the cover. I would do this repeatedly and she enjoyed the game, always finding the wing and bringing it back to me. When we had Brittany puppies, Pepsi's ability to find any wing that people could hide in the alfalfa field was a big help in selling her pups. It was also great practice and Pepsi developed into the best retriever of the Brittanys I have owned.

Pepsi was also one of the most obedient of my dogs and it almost got her killed. I was fly fishing on the Fall River in southeastern Idaho and Pepsi had somehow climbed up out of the steep little river canyon and walked out on the road bridge a little upriver from where I was fishing. I could not find her and I kept calling until suddenly a Brittany came falling through the air from the bridge in a drop of about 50 feet until she hit the river, barely missing a large protruding boulder. She had jumped over the solid bridge railing trying to get back to me. That was some kind of splash!

Brook retrieving a rooster in 2012.

Ch. 46. Retrieving and misleading

It was late in the pheasant season in the mid-1970s when, travelling on a gravel road, I saw two roosters on an area of private land. The posted sign said no hunting but I decided it didn't hurt to ask. The landowner denied me permission but as we visited he changed his mind and decided to go with me on the hunt. In this situation I am always hoping the person is a safe hunter.

We walked about 200 yards from his house to reach a dry marsh bounded by harvested corn on one side—a great looking spot for mid-season pheasants. Dry wetlands were the norm in this drought year. The wetland covered about two acres and had a mixture of giant burreed, dock weed, river bulrush, and a variety of other types of wetland plants. My Brittany, Pepsi, was quickly onto birds in the dense cover near the edge of the dry marsh and she pointed a rooster right off. The landowner swung on the bird as it flushed and dropped it with a broken wing in a small opening at about 25 yards. The pheasant sprinted into the wetland cover with the dog soon after it. Pepsi went about 20 yards in the direction the bird headed and then did a sharp left turn and headed off to the edge of the wetland. I still remember the landowner telling me to "get that dog over here, the pheasant went this way!" He was most insistent I get that disobedient dog back to help find the bird while Pepsi was most persistent in trailing off in another direction. In his exasperation at my dog and while yelling at her he suddenly stopped as he spotted Pepsi headed back from about 100 yards away with the bird in her mouth. I didn't need to say anything else to the landowner to get him to trust the dog on the birds we took after that. Pheasants can certainly mislead your educated guesses so you best trust the dog's sense of smell.

In one instance in dense grass cover my dog ran to a downed bird 20 yards ahead of me, then turned and ran back toward me missing me by about two yards and heading in the opposite direction. By that time I had learned that the dog knew much more than I did and in that case she did bring the bird back from an area totally opposite of where I thought the bird would go. How could that pheasant run through the grass within two yards of me without me detecting it?

In my experience, the best retrievers are dogs bred specifically to retrieve such as Labrador retrievers or Springer spaniels. My Brittanys have found most of the downed and running birds but they have not performed as well as some retrievers I have watched while hunting with friends. Some of the retrievers are uncanny in their ability to find a running and wounded pheasant even in spots loaded with scent from other pheasants.

I've also known of a couple of gun dogs that found downed or running birds but always refused to pick them up. One of my frequent hunting and fishing companions, Gary Peterson, had a small Brittany named Pasu (Lakota Sioux for nose) that pointed beautifully and would run down a crippled bird and hold it with her paws but would not retrieve it. One year (1983) when Gary was on sabbatical from SDSU I took care of his dog in his absence and hunted her, in part because my dog had been killed that previous summer. I had gone out dove hunting and shot a mourning dove that fell in a pond. I was trying to figure out how to get it since Pasu did not retrieve. Pasu looked at me, looked at the dove, and then went out into the shallow pond and retrieved it—the only bird retrieve she ever made or would make in her life. I am completely convinced that this dog knew how to retrieve but was not going to do so for a perfectly healthy human that could do the job without help. The dove in the pond was a situation where Pasu saw I had to have help. I continued to hunt with Pasu that season and she never did retrieve a single pheasant, grouse, or other game bird. It's obvious, hunting dogs are pretty intelligent.

Ch. 47. Bird dogs—warm, friendly, and mobile remote sensors

At South Dakota State University (SDSU) a close friend, Vic Myers, headed up the Remote Sensing Institute for many years. Remote sensing often requires the use of high altitude or space photography to evaluate landscapes; it involves always-improving and impressive technology, especially in the military. Although not exactly a standard type of remote sensor, gun dogs in their own way have highly impressive sensory skills for detecting scent that humans can hardly comprehend. Hunting dogs often do an impressive job of sensing birds at a distance using scent, certainly as impressive as some of the most advanced military technology. Vic Myers hunted over my gun dogs many times—I'm sure he agreed.

South of Brookings I was on a Waterfowl Production Area (WPA) hunting the edge of a wide grass strip around a wetland with my gun dog. Next to me and parallel to the general direction my dog was working was a recently plowed and barren area of soil where U.S. Fish and Wildlife Service personnel intended to seed native grass cover. About 80 yards away a weedy fence line bordered the far side of the tilled soil. As I worked the edge of the cover my dog held its head high into the southeast wind blowing toward us across the tilled field. Continuing to hold her head high (no bird scent on the tilled ground) and into the wind, she turned to walk across the tilled field to the weedy fence line at which point she froze on point. She was holding three or four hens in that fence line and I was astonished that she picked up the scent at that distance and led me to those birds.

On a cool early November day in the 1970s I was hunting the cover along the railroad tracks several miles west of Volga in eastern South Dakota. The railroad tracks were about six to eight feet higher than the right-of-way in the place I was hunting. My dog was working at normal speed when she stopped and rose up on her hind feet like I have seldom seen a Brittany do while hunting. She was scenting something in the crosswind blowing from the other side of the railroad tracks so I took the cue and followed her over the railroad bed onto the other side of the railroad right-of-way. Sure enough, she had a group of pheasants detected and provided a staunch point on what turned out to be two roosters and several hens that flushed close to both me and the dog.

When I was younger, especially in my 30s, I was more likely to purposely force my dog ("Get in there!") and myself into heavy cover, especially dense cattail patches, to hunt pheasants. With experience I began to trust the dog more and I let my Brittanys walk the downwind edges of heavy cover. I would watch the dog and stay within or close to shooting range when she headed into the heavy cover on hot scent. That saved hunter wear and tear and worked just as well as pushing thick cattails or other heavy cover much of the time. The dog often picks up the scent of birds hiding in the cover or that just moved into the cover and will then lead you to them. I still sometimes push the dog to hunt heavy cover if I think the wind direction is not allowing the dog to pick up scent or if I know birds are holding tight under snowy conditions. However, as much as possible I let the dogs do the work and lead me to the birds with those unique sensing abilities.

One reason I enjoy hunting either alone or at a distance from my hunting companion or companions is that I can often be more effective if I follow the dog instead of having a preplanned route when hunting an area. I usually have a general direction I want to go and mosey in that direction but if the dog is hot on birds I abandon plans and follow the dog. This has often greatly changed my plans in terms of how I was going to hunt. In some cases dogs will even seemingly turn and go right back into an area you just finished hunting. I'm never surprised anymore since such a move has often resulted in pinning down a tricky rooster. Just remember, a good hunting dog has olfactory sensing capabilities that you will never have so you need to watch hunting dogs carefully and understand the communications they send your way.

Ch. 48. Hey boss—pay attention

While fly fishing in Alaska with my friend, Gary Peterson, a coastal brown bear (same species as a grizzly) showed up above us on a steep bank and quickly spotted the sockeye salmon that the guy a few yards from us was fighting into the shallows. The angler should have given the fish more line, dropped his rod, and moved away but instead started running toward us and others nearby with the splashing fish and the bear trailing. The bear soon nabbed the sockeye salmon. I figure that is the only time I will ever see an angler with an enormous bear on the end of his fly line—even though it was for only a few seconds. Anyway, at that moment I was keenly alert as were the other people nearby because of the surprise visit by the bear.

I share this bear experience because it reminds me of how important it is to be alert and thinking ahead when you are hunting upland birds. You will not likely have a grizzly bear visit you to keep you alert except possibly if you are after spruce grouse or even pheasants (a few spots) in a place like western Montana. Nevertheless, staying alert while hunting with a dog makes a big difference in success and is important to a hunter's safety. Every experienced hunter has known the feeling of not watching the hunting dog closely enough, not watching their tail and other cues, and of knowing hard earned opportunities for some good shooting have been lost because of not paying attention.

If each of my gun dogs could have talked to me and tried to train me better as a hunter I think they might tell me to pay attention and be alert on the hunt from the start to the end of the day. Sometimes you get out of the car and action starts while you are still thinking about something at work or home or otherwise not paying attention. One day northwest of Brookings Jack Connelly and I stopped to hunt a beautiful private area of grass-forb cover. We got our dogs out of the vehicle and, while I was still getting my hunting vest on and shotgun loaded, Jack informed me my dog was on point about 30 yards away. I was not ready and definitely clueless until Jack got my attention. Jack walked over to my dog, flushing the rooster pheasant at close range as I watched the action. Glad someone was alert!

Most of my problems in missing good opportunities come from not paying close enough attention to the dog or being a little lazy about checking out a spot of cover where she seems moderately interested. One day while hunting sharp-tailed grouse I walked away from a dense accumulation of tumbleweeds along a fence line even though I saw the dog turn and go back to check it out further. I knew no grouse could possibly be in that bunch of weeds since three of us had stopped and visited noisily about 50 yards away. As I walked away, I looked back to see where my dog was in time to see one of my hunting companions standing ready by that cover with my dog staunchly on point. As the flock of about a dozen sharptails flushed, it was too late for me but not for my hunting companion who had noted the dog's interest and stayed with her. Unfortunately, I'm still repeating similar scenes every fall.

Recently, my dog Brook locked onto a solid point in native grass cover along the Missouri River bottoms. I especially remember the beautiful point by Brook because of how I fumbled the ball. I walked up on the dog and a long-tailed, colorful pheasant rose into the wind, holding there momentarily it seemed so I could take the easy shot. I swung, pulled the trigger, and nothing happened. I had not been alert when I got out of the car and had forgotten to jack a shell into the chamber. That rooster left me with a mental photo that I remember more than any of the rooster pheasants I successfully bagged that year. I know, pretty dumb move but I'm sure I am not alone. And I ended up with only one pheasant that day.

Years ago Marcia stitched me a little wall hanging with my dog Pepsi on point and a pheasant flushing a few feet ahead of the dog. On the wall hanging were the words "Les and Pepsi." If Pepsi could talk she would have probably complained about the days I failed to stay alert and attentive when she was getting close on pheasants or grouse. I'm still working at that lesson on being alert and attentive while hunting and in several other aspects of life. A penchant for daydreaming has its price.

Hey you guys, pay attention! I've got a bird here!
Brook in 2012 on a friends place north of Onida, South Dakota.

Ch. 49. Running with the dog

When I was in my 30s and even through my 40s I would regularly run with the dog when she got on pheasant scent. One day I took a friend from Pierre, Tony Dean, out pheasant hunting near Brookings and we spent quite a bit of the day jogging along behind the dog. Tony later said he had heard of having dogs run with the hunter but he had never thought of the hunter running with the dog. That was classic Tony Dean humor. I took the hint and slowed down my pace. Still, sometimes a quick dash with the dog can help hold a rooster that you just can't seem to pin down. Running on a regular basis carrying a loaded shotgun is risky and, as you get older, a good way to trigger a heart attack. If you step in a badger digging or other hole it is also a good way to detach ligaments or otherwise injure yourself. I have learned to slow down although I still rush to get close to the dog when I know it is hot on a bird or on point. Today, at over 70, I usually depend on the dog to hold the bird on point until I get there.

Tony Dean died unexpectedly in October of 2008 and left an enormous gap in the efforts to conserve wildlife habitats in South Dakota. He was a well-known outdoor media personality and was often instrumental in stopping unwise legislation or other actions that would have destroyed wetlands, public grasslands (especially national grasslands), and other important habitats. His voice is greatly needed and missed by those who value wildlife and wild places in South Dakota and the upper Midwest.

Ch. 50. Get back—it's a skunk!

On a beautiful but subfreezing late November day (sometime in the early 1990s) I was hunting south of Brookings with my friend Gary Peterson. As Gary expectantly approached his Brittany spaniel that had locked up solid on point, neither of us had any anticipation of what was really about to happen. Gary did not see or smell the skunk his dog was pointing in time to call him off and the dog got the full brunt of skunk spray. Direct hit at close range!

The putrid-sweet, pungent smell was overwhelming and was the worst "skunking" I have known. The dog was so heavily sprayed that I recall it having a visible greenish film covering parts of the body hit most directly. We did not have anything on hand for treating the dog. We continued to hunt for a while but Gary, who had driven out to meet me at this hunting spot, decided he had best get back to Brookings and clean the dog up with the standard mix of hydrogen peroxide, baking soda, and detergent.

Gary was driving the new family van and was well aware that his wife Pam would not appreciate the vehicle smelling like skunk for weeks—neither would Gary. To avoid smelling up the van more than absolutely necessary Gary tied his dog kennel to the overhead rails on top of the van, put his dog in the kennel, and drove the dog home. With the open wire front on the kennel, it was a cold ride for the dog but helped keep the car clear of the more extreme levels of skunk smell. A few weeks later Gary and I were talking to a friend, Bob Dallman, about the cold temperatures. Bob laughed and said something like "you think you guys are feeling the cold." Then he unknowingly commented about a pet owner that he had seen drive by with a dog in a kennel strapped to the top of a vehicle in subfreezing weather. We ask a couple of questions and soon recognized that it was Gary with his "skunky" dog on top of that vehicle. I recently reminisced with both of these friends about the skunking, the car top ride, and Bob's comments. That skunk really left us with some fun memories!

Finding Paradise in South Dakota

In another interesting situation, we had brought in a guest speaker, Joe Ball, from the University of Montana to talk to students and faculty in a late afternoon seminar on a waterfowl related topic. Joe enjoyed hunting and we took a few hours before his seminar lecture to hunt pheasants. Midway through the hunt Joe's German shorthair pup (Hoover) slammed into an awesome rock-solid point at the edge of dense, chest-high grass cover. It was one of Hoover's first points and Joe was especially proud. Nothing flushed as he walked around in the spot where Hoover was pointing so Joe started pushing the vegetation aside. We could not smell a skunk and we thought it had to be a rooster. It was not! Joe first felt a liquid running from his hairline, into his left eyebrow and left ear. He even remembers a greenish-yellow liquid dripping onto his mustache and a strong minty/musty odor. He recalls thinking the smell was not that objectionable at first. These descriptive words are from Joe's account. We never did see the skunk and neither dog got sprayed. The experience apparently left a deep impression on Joe's mind.

We ended the hunt because of the skunking and because we had to get back for the lecture. We had no hydrogen peroxide, baking soda, tomato juice or other materials to help clean up Joe. I was definitely concerned about how to get him back to Brookings without making the cab of my pickup smell like skunk spray. I ended up covering the seat of my pickup with an old jacket and hunting shirt and we headed back to Brookings. Joe tried to clean up as much as possible at the motel with tomato juice and hydrogen peroxide. We barely made it to his guest lecture in time! It made for a fun introduction of Dr. Ball as seminar speaker that afternoon. I tried to control any chuckling or laughing but it was tough. Joe has an excellent memory and has let me know he does not "forgive and forget easily." As his wife Sue will attest, it took a month to get rid of the smell in his mustache and ear. The smell within my pickup also lingered for a similar time span and who knows how long the smell lasted in the motel room.

When I lived in South Dakota I usually encountered several skunks each year but in most cases I could smell or see the skunk and get the dog away before she got sprayed. I have never been personally sprayed with more than a fine mist associated with a close call. I did get my father-in-law fairly well sprayed on the boots and legs during a pheasant hunt. Still, my dogs have taken a solid hit fewer than five or six times in 41 years of intensive pheasant hunting in South Dakota. A couple of times I have spotted the dog pointing a skunks rear end (and with the skunks tail raised) at only two or three feet distance and have still managed to call the dog back without her getting sprayed. It seems like most skunks are reluctant to spray a potential enemy. With the encounters I have had over the years I have begun carrying a small bucket with dish detergent, a bottle of hydrogen peroxide, and baking soda to treat the dogs if sprayed. I have also used anti-bacterial soaps to remove the smell. A couple of cleanings may be necessary if it is a house dog. I recommend you carry skunk treatments plus water and a bucket in the vehicle on upland bird hunts in South Dakota. The recipe can be easily found on the Internet.

Ch. 51. A bad guy kills my Brittany

Dogs often die for strange reasons but the loss of my first Brittany, Pepsi, was the strangest of all dog deaths. At 10.5 years old Pepsi was shot with an arrow by a deranged college student during the summer when she got through the fence in our back yard in Brookings and entered the abutting property associated with the university's married student housing. Our family was out of town but our daughter Margo (a senior in high school) had stayed home to work and was caring for Pepsi. Sadly, Margo was on our elevated deck when Pepsi came home with an arrow in her side and died in front of her. Our family friend, Gary Peterson, buried Pepsi on a private farm (Cal's) near town where we had often hunted. One of the police officers in town who later became police chief, Dennis Falken, had a daughter in high school that was friends with my daughter Margo. Officer Falken was quite upset about someone shooting my dog with an arrow and went door to door in the married student housing area questioning people. He was professionally knowledgeable about how to recognize when someone was guilty—he found the culprit. That was not the only time that Dennis helped our family and we still appreciate him.

Pepsi was an especially friendly dog and the guy who killed her could give no reason for his actions. The city judge collected a fine from this crazy, somewhat older student and gave $400 to me to purchase my next Brittany pup, Rascal. I did not meet the person who killed Pepsi and it is probably best that way. I did not want to even know his name. This person was suspected of poisoning at least two other hunting dogs and had done other crazy things like sending letters to federal and state officials requesting a waiver of all hunting licenses so he could kill unlimited deer and feed himself; his argument was that this would save the government money as he, his wife, and children would no longer need food stamps. He also sent a similar letter to officials requesting blanket permission to place salt licks and hunt deer over them. Sorry to say, I think this weird individual was studying to become a high school teacher. I hope he did not finish his degree. I'm very sorry for his wife.

Losing my dog in this way was a tough lesson to learn but there are a few jerks out there that will shoot, poison, or otherwise try to hurt a pet just out of sheer cruelty. Be careful with your hunting dog and don't assume others appreciate hunting dogs regardless of how friendly and well behaved the dog. Be especially cautious hunting near rural roads where drivers in a rush too often make no attempt to slow down even with a dog on or alongside the road.

Ch. 52. Gun dog and a pet mallard

My most recent adult Brittany, Brook (died October 2014), did a good job on most retrieves and was a big help in finding downed pheasants. When I hunted ducks she also liked to retrieve even though she was a poor swimmer. Unfortunately, I had no idea how one could teach a dog how to dog paddle in the correct manner. Perhaps I should have swam with her to illustrate the appropriate dog paddle stroke. When retrieving in water, Brook dog paddled in some weird, struggling manner but still managed to stay afloat and to slowly get to birds in deeper water.

In 2008 I brought home a mallard duckling of mixed wild and domestic parentage and reared it in my yard. Two of my grandchildren, Bryce and Grace, had helped me bait and net the duckling at a city park where they were having problems with too many domestic ducks—the children had a great interest in keeping this bird for a pet in our yard. At first I thought the dog would kill the duck but Brook recognized the duck was a pet and they soon became friends and hung out together. Grace named the duck Puddles. The mallard had several white wing primaries (outer flight feathers) and, when old enough, could fly quite well. Puddles was about the same size as a wild mallard when he matured.

Marcia warned me that this relationship would ruin my dog forever for hunting and especially for retrieving. As things turned out, the duck began to become very aggressive and seemed to dominate my 40-pound dog, chasing, pecking, and pulling hair from Brook at times. The duck was so aggressive that a neighbor called one day to tell me Puddles had flown over to their place and had their 20-25 pound dog cornered and terrified in their yard.

Brook would occasionally retaliate by grabbing Puddles in retrieving fashion and carrying him around the yard for a couple of minutes. Still, the duck simply attacked again when the dog set him down unharmed. At other times they lay together, Puddles cuddled up against the dogs belly, like they were great friends. I think Brook just put up with the duck because she knew it was our pet.

Puddles (the duck) was constantly pulling out Brooks hair by the beak full.

During this pet duck episode, we brought home a six-week old Brittany, Coco, that my daughter Margo had us pick up and hold for her until she could travel from California to take it home in about a month. We were especially concerned about the aggressive duck seriously injuring the young puppy. In fact, the duck stalked and would have viciously attacked the pup if given a chance. We were careful to keep the puppy away from Puddles. However, when Coco was about nine weeks of age, the duck got his chance and viciously attacked the puppy before we could interfere. We got a big surprise as did Puddles! Instead of an injured Coco, the puppy reversed the attack and aggressively chased the duck, nipping at the duck and ripping at the tail feathers. After that, we had a three-way circus with Puddles attacking the adult dog Brook and the puppy (Coco) stalking and attacking Puddles.

When I went hunting with Brook the next fall she was still the same hunter as before we got the pet duck. She retrieved pheasants, grouse, and ducks in normal fashion. I sometimes wondered what the dog thought when she retrieved drake mallards that looked so similar to the pet we had at home.

Brook would occasionally retaliate by softly grabbing Puddles in retrieving fashion and carrying him around the yard.

Coco at 9 weeks reversed the aggressor role and began attacking puddles the duck (in drab midsummer plumage).

Ch. 53. Gun dogs in the doghouse

I suppose this list could be quite long but I will just share a couple of problems I had with two of my gun dogs. Both were still great hunters and fun dogs but they just did not do so well in the house. My second Brittany, Rascal, was from a line out of Pierre South Dakota that may have been the best hunting stock of all of my Brittanys. As a 12-week old "house trained" pup I put her in an enclosed portion of the basement with a cement floor where I thought she could not get in trouble while I was at work. However, I received a phone call from my wife Marcia about 4 p.m. (early 1980s) when she got home from teaching at Brookings High School. She told me "my" dog had destroyed the land line phone (no cell phones then) on the wall. I had never imagined that Rascal might pull the phone down and chew it up like a tasty bone. It was also a first "phone chewing" for our local phone company.

A couple of months later I had left this puppy on a leash on a stair landing by the back door. Marcia called me at work to tell me the dog had redesigned the new linoleum on the landing. I got home to find she had torn the new linoleum from the floor like tearing a piece of paper in half. We worked further trying to integrate Rascal into the family but she ended up spending much of her time in a nice kennel outside with visits in the house. She was a great hunting dog with an incredible nose and a beautiful point but she had a way of getting into trouble so she was only allowed in the house as a guest.

My third Brittany, Kali, was given to me by Chuck Scalet, our department head for most of the years I worked at SDSU. He had bred his male Brittany to another dog of high pedigree in Minnesota and had a free pup coming. Thanks, Chuck, for a great hunting dog!.

Kali was a fast learner and an effective hunter and probably my largest Brittany at about 50 pounds. She did have some unusual characteristics that I learned of after the owner-pet bonding was already accomplished. One of those strange characteristics was that she gulped instead of lapped water like normal dogs. She would stick her entire face and most of her head in the water bucket or pan and push water all over the floor. She seldom seemed to lap water with her tongue. Perhaps we could have just watered her outdoors but she had another strange behavior that kept her from being a regular house dog.

When Kali approached you or you approached her she would get excited to see you and would spin around in tight circles like she was chasing her short tail. She would consistently make several tight circles before deciding to settle down. This behavior was very pronounced and inborn and I have never seen it this severe in other dogs. She still was allowed to visit us in the house but spent most of her time in her kennel and in the fenced back yard, often staring at us through the sliding glass doors to the deck. I got extremely attached to this dog over the 10 years she lived until she died of an undiagnosed illness.

A springer spaniel scaled an 8 foot high dog kennel fence and left Rascal pregnant with these cute black and white pups. Our children (Ryan here) loved each litter of pups.

Ch. 54. Walking my hunting dog—The amorous Pyrenees

If you have a hunting dog it is especially important to get it out on regular walks, if possible every day. Such walks can lead to unanticipated experiences—I will share this one.

In the early spring of 2011 I took my female Brittany Brook on a hike up the Hobble Creek trail near our home in Springville Utah. I love to walk this trail because the surrounding mountains are beautiful and I can look at certain pools in the creek to count the brown trout and check their size. I occasionally see a trout that looks to be close to 20 inches, though the best brown trout I have caught on my fly rod in that small creek was 18 inches.

I parked about two miles from my house near the paved Hobble Creek trail and had walked back down the canyon. Less than a half mile down the trail I heard something running toward us and turned just as a large male Pyrenees approached—no owner was around. I had left my dog leash in my vehicle since there was still snow on the ground and I figured no one else would be on the trail.

I quickly realized to my dismay that my dog must be starting estrus as the Pyrenees was earnestly trying to breed her. I ran after both dogs but neither would cooperate. When they slowed down I reached the two dogs in time to knock the male off of my Brittany just as he was trying to impregnate her. I grabbed Brook by the collar and with the other hand and my feet and legs began fighting off the enormous (about 90 to 100 pounds) but friendly Pyrenees.

Moving towards a nearby spot where a small cement canal went under the paved trail, I used the drop off into the ditch to hold my dogs rear portions over the edge and try and keep the male at bay. I could not control the amorous Pyrenees and he was determined to breed Brook. It must have looked like a real circus. The enthusiastic Pyrenees would go down into the shallow ditch to try and get to her. I would then pull the dog back up but the male quickly would come back on top of the path and try to mount Brook. I would again move the rear of my dog so she was partly hanging off the bridge and the male would move back into the shallow ditch to try from that angle. I continued to fight him off but he was powerful and persistent and I was beginning to tire. This same pattern went on and on for what seemed like about 20 minutes. It was cold but I was dripping with sweat from fighting this determined male. He showed no indication that he would bite me, he just wanted the female. I called for help several times hoping the owner might be somewhere near or that other hikers might come along. No use, no one could hear me.

In desperation I put Brook (about 40 pounds) on my shoulders and wrapped her around my neck to get away but the amorous Pyrenees then put his paws right up on my neck, shoulders, or back and began to circle on his two legs. Again, fortunately, he seemed to have no tendency to bite. Nothing I tried was working at all. I continued to kick at him and knock him off of me but he always jumped right back up. It looked like Brook and I were dancing with him. I was tiring rapidly and I had by then twisted one of my legs and my foot during this awkward dance with the huge dog. Finally I decided I had to get a weapon so I looked around and spotted a pile of dead limbs about 40 yards away. I packed Brook over to the pile of limbs with her still on my shoulders, picked up a limb about 4 inches in diameter, and began swinging it at the Pyrenees. He did not like the limb and after a couple of close calls backed off a little.

Putting Brook on the ground, I began pulling her along by holding her collar but she did not really cooperate either and was just as interested as the male. I carried the limb in one hand and would swing at the dog each time he approached. In this manner I had walked about half way back to the car when the owner showed up and took control of his Pyrenees. Brook did not get pregnant even though at one point I was not sure I had knocked the Pyrenees off fast enough. I was so glad to get back to the car and to not end up with Pyrenees x Brittany puppies. Even though I hike and work out every day, at 70 years of age that was a tough situation to handle. It would have been a challenge even when I was much younger.

Finding Paradise in South Dakota

The Pyrenees put his paws right up on my neck, shoulders, or back and began to circle on his two legs. It looked like we were dancing.

Ch. 55. Pitbull attack on Thanksgiving

I thought I would let you know what happened to my Brittany Brook on a visit to California as a warning that you might want to carry some pepper spray when walking your hunting dog. My daughter Margo and I were walking the trail in Folsom Lake State Park on Thanksgiving Day with our two Brittanys, Brook and Coco. Two fairly rough looking 25-to 30-year-old guys with unleashed pitbulls were loitering near the path. The larger pitbull suddenly attacked Brook repeatedly for what seemed like about 10 minutes, each time biting down and holding on tight. When he attacked he bit down tight on her throat and neck twice and once bit down and held and tore her ear. My friendly Brittany was on a leash as required in the park and was completely docile—she was yelping for her life throughout the attack. The attack was unprovoked and vicious. I was right in the middle of it as were the two guys and even Margo although I tried to keep her away. The second pitbull also approached and bared his fangs at me but did not attack.

We could not break off the last attack on Brooks ear and it lasted a long time before a hiker came by and said to choke the pitbull with the leash. That got him off but too late to prevent three major punctures on the back of the neck and another deep puncture in the side of the throat. The attack would have killed my daughters much smaller Brittany. One of Brooks ears lost some pieces and somehow the pitbull bit her back foot and detached a pad. She was laid up for 14 days but recovered. The two guys gave me false contact and identification information. I ended up with a $450 vet bill. With the oak woods all around, two loitering guys with pitbulls, and a good chance they were pushing drugs, we might be fortunate we did not press further for ID proof. I might have taken a picture if I had a phone but that may have set off worse violence against my daughter and me.

The two guys slipped away quickly but I did not follow them down the wooded trail as I thought it could escalate and I would be on the losing end. It was a tough day for a nine-year old Brittany and for my daughter Margo and me. No matter how much some people tell me they love pitbulls, given this attack and the attacks I have been told of or read about on several people (including fatal attacks on children and adults), I'm now a fan of banning this aggressive breed. I now carry bear spray on my hikes and I am more wary of any large dogs I see running loose, especially pitbulls. I'm even leery of pitbulls on a leash.

Ch. 56. Other interesting encounters for dogs

In the 1970s I thought my Brittany Pepsi was pretty special in terms of finding and pointing pheasants and grouse. One spring, we had a visiting speaker in our department at South Dakota State University (SDSU) who wanted to watch my dog point pheasants. We went out to a federal Waterfowl Production Area in early April and began walking the cover. After we had walked a few hundred yards I was proud as I watched Pepsi lock onto a beautiful point. That is, until I found she was embarrassingly pointing, of all things, a painted turtle that had moved out of its normal wetland habitat onto the uplands. My guest commented that I had a "terrific turtle pointer."

When Pepsi was just six months old I took her on her first hunt (for grouse) and she kept pointing grassland songbirds like meadowlarks. I badly wanted her to point a grouse so I could shoot the first bird over my own dog. I recall her locking up on point in river-break country near the Missouri River only to have a vesper sparrow flush as I walked up to her. I yelled something like "come on Pepsi" in an unhappy tone and kicked the shrub by my feet. However, as I kicked the shrub a single sharp-tailed grouse burst from the spot she was pointing, about two feet from where the sparrow flew up. I was off balance and missed the grouse and a great chance to reward the dog with her first bird. It would have also been my first sharp-tailed grouse. I praised her and we soon got into plenty of sharp-tailed grouse that she was able to point and retrieve. Since then I have gotten used to Brittanys pointing songbirds when they are young and even flash pointing meadowlarks and some other grassland songbirds as adults. Experienced pointers usually only hold points on songbirds momentarily.

On a late November day in the 1970s I was hunting with a friend, Jerran Flinders, who was visiting as a guest speaker from Brigham Young University. We were getting points on pheasants but we also got three unexpected points on raccoons. At any rate, in all three cases Pepsi held off from attacking which was probably good for her health. Large raccoons can be tough fighters. Raccoons are overly abundant in eastern South Dakota and have benefited by eating foods like corn and by denning in old buildings, culverts, and silos. I knew the pelt prices (about $25 each then) were good and I shot and collected the raccoons. I would like to see a lot fewer raccoons as was the case in earlier centuries when native prairies predominated on the landscape.

In the 1990s I had asked a farmer friend south of Brookings if I could hunt pheasants and then ended up with a point on a raccoon. I collected the raccoon only to find out from my friend (Larry) that his kids had a pet raccoon. I don't think he liked the pet raccoon that much plus it turned out that the one I brought in was a wild raccoon. Glad for that!

All of my dogs have pointed cottontails with pretty serious intent. It has not been a problem and I know some hunters are after cottontails at the same time they are hunting pheasants. Rarely, I have also had points on domestic cats (away from the farmstead), mice, and even porcupines. The porcupines were along cover associated with intermittent streams in western South Dakota. Jack Connelly, hunting in the same west-river spots, seems to find porcupines quite regularly. Maybe German shorthairs are just better porcupine dogs than Brittanys. All porcupine encounters were in areas with mainly prairie grouse but you could run into them in West River pheasant habitat.

Ch. 57. Etiquette if you are invited to hunt over a bird dog

I sometimes will take one other person with me to hunt over my Brittany and rarely two. The more people over a single dog the more difficult it is to hunt. If you do hunt with another person over their gun dog be sure to avoid trying to command or direct the dog in any way. I tell people upfront to avoid commanding or talking to my dog while she is hunting. If you don't like how someone works their dog then I strongly suggest you not go with them or get your own hunting dog. You will not likely be invited back if you command the dog or make disparaging remarks.

On one such experience I took a friend of a friend with me and my dog on a pheasant hunt. I'm sure he was a fine individual but the arrangement worked out poorly. This person was an assertive individual who had hunted bobwhite quail over gun dogs. He let me know right away that I needed to bring my dog back and continue to work certain spots with heavy cover and plentiful pheasant tracks (in the snow). That approach can work but I knew this spot and I was pretty sure the birds were moving well ahead of us. He also told me what a well-trained dog would do and repeatedly made it clear my Brittany did not fit that category and was in need of much training. I'm sure this person left thinking that I had a poorly trained dog even though he saw some of the running pheasants flush far ahead. Since that experience, I sometimes tell people that go hunting with me that my dog is not professionally trained but that she gets plenty of pheasants if you stay with her. If you like hunting with your dog, then that is all that really counts. Each year I get lots of fantastic points and retrieves from my "untrained" dog.

Often when I take a person with my dog they will have difficulty being in the right spot because they do not recognize when the dog is "birdy" and they lag back or to the side too far. When the dog does point or flush a bird, they are often too far away to get up to the bird and get a good shot. Hunting dogs communicate by distinct behaviors when they have found hot scent. If I tell an accompanying hunter that the dog is "birdy" the hunter will initially hurry and get close to the dog. However, bird dogs sometimes repeatedly get "birdy" without flushing birds, or, for pointers, without getting a solid point on a bird; in the case of pheasants, the birds have often run ahead. Hunting dogs will also move in different directions and even backtrack after birds, confusing a hunter less experienced with your gun dog. It can be difficult and frustrating to keep telling an accompanying hunter or hunters to keep up and be alert. And of course, as soon you stop paying close attention the dog points or flushes the bird.

 I watch my dog closely (if visible) and when she is hot or goes on point I move quickly to get within shotgun range. In taller cover you may have to watch the movement of the vegetation, listen for the dog movements, or listen for something like a bell or beeper signal. The movements and behavior of a gun dog forewarn you that a bird is close. If I take another hunter, I have gotten so I just let them learn the hard way that they need to pay attention to the tail and head movements and general behavior of the dog. Regardless of whether you are working the dog close or at a greater distance, you need to be able to interpret when the dog is "birdy." Even if it is a pointing dog, other behaviors usually forewarn you before the dog actually goes on point.

Part VI. Related memories and distractions

Ch. 58. Ducks and geese—lots of 'em

It is not unusual to run into substantial numbers of ducks and geese in eastern and central South Dakota during the pheasant hunt, especially during peak migration prior to freeze up. These waterfowl concentrations can definitely be so impressive as to distract you from the pheasant hunt. Many times I have stopped to watch Canada geese, white fronts, lesser snow geese, mallards, and other waterfowl fly over—sometimes flock after flock. At times I remember my father-in-law Ruel's voice as he joshed me about watching the circling ducks and geese when I needed to stay focused on pheasants. It can be an incredible sight if you like to watch or hunt waterfowl. It always gives me a thrill and adds to the enjoyment of being in South Dakota. Pheasants, prairie grouse, and waterfowl—that is the essence of fall In South Dakota to me!

When I was a South Dakota resident I sometimes kept waders and a bag of decoys in my pickup while pheasant hunting in case I saw an exceptional situation with large numbers of ducks setting their wings and dropping into a wetland near where I was hunting. One November day in the late 1990s, I was hunting pheasants on private land about a half hour from Brookings and having good success. A brisk northwest wind was gusting up to 20-25 miles per hour. A large semipermanent wetland where I sometimes hunted ducks was in the middle of the section and I soon noticed that flocks of mallards were frequently dropping into this wetland. It was very distracting to the pheasant hunt. This hemimarsh had the classic arrangement of about half emergent cattail and bulrush and half open water. After freeze up, I often hunted the wetland for pheasants that were attracted to the dense cattail stands.

I tried to ignore the ducks and kept hunting pheasants for another hour, but finally decided two pheasants were plenty. I could not stand to pass up this chance for mallards any longer! At that point I went back to the vehicle, got out the waders, and headed for the marsh. I waded through the muck in the 80-acre marsh to reach a good stand of cattails upwind from open water, flushing hundreds of ducks on the way out. I put my dog on a muskrat house in easy view of any ducks that might decoy and tossed out fewer than a dozen decoys. Ducks were landing near me before I could even get out the decoys. Getting into heavy emergent cover, I watched as large flocks of mallards dropped out of the gray sky toward the marsh. I let each flock of mallards approach until they were hanging over the decoys, picked out drakes, and soon finished a great day of both pheasant and duck hunting. Apparently the orange and white Brittany in plain view on the muskrat house did not scare the flocks of mallards, at least on that day.

Waterfowl can become very distracting during upland bird hunts in East River South Dakota.

That reminds me of my long-time friend Ken Higgins, a colleague in my department at SDSU, who recalls some interesting traditions for waterfowl hunting. Apparently some of Ken's friends in North Dakota traditionally chose a warm day in the fall and dressed up in a white shirt and tie for a duck hunt on their favorite duck pass. Ken said ducks are not afraid of white and that makes sense with all the egrets, snow geese, gulls, and other white birds hanging around marshes. Ken also liked to go on an annual coot hunt. He even published an article in the *North Dakota Outdoors* magazine titled something like "The incredible, edible coot." Ken says they are pretty good cooked up in a smoker, marinated, and even fried.

In another situation in mid-November in the 1990s, I found myself in 30-35 mile per hour winds when I arrived at a favorite private farm south of Brookings where I had planned to pheasant hunt. Large flocks of lesser snow geese were flying low from the west into one of the harvested cornfields on the property and, though I could not see the field from my location, the sounds of the geese calling and gabbling indicated that thousands were already on the ground and gorging themselves with waste corn. With the blustery conditions and so many live geese on the ground for decoys I could not pass up this chance—pheasants could wait on this windy day. I took my dog and worked through some low spots in an area of switchgrass (CRP) to get downwind of the snow geese and under the arriving flocks.

As I headed for the area below the arriving flocks of geese my Brittany pointed a couple of roosters at close range but I did not chance shooting and scaring the geese. With the howling wind and thousands of noisy geese it probably would not have mattered. It all worked well as I soon experienced the excitement of having snow geese flying overhead at 15 to 20 yards and was able to take a few white and blue phase birds home. That's the nature of South Dakota in the fall. For hunters there is so much to do, so much to see.

If you want to hunt ducks along with pheasants or grouse, nonresidents need to apply for a 10-day waterfowl license in the late spring or early summer.

Ch. 59. High winds, ducks, and corn shucks

It was thanksgiving week, a few years before I retired from SDSU and moved to Utah with my wife, Marcia. Late November is a great time of year to hunt pheasants; if freeze up is late it can also be a peak time for late migrating ducks, mainly mallards. That year daily high temperatures near Brookings were still enough above freezing to keep most of the marshes ice free. Although there had been considerable rain in the last few days, there had been little or no snow. It was an unusually warm fall. To the north, the Canadian provinces, North Dakota, and some of the northern edge of South Dakota had been hit with subfreezing temperatures, snow, and iced-up wetlands. Mallards had begun moving into the areas west of Brookings in large numbers.

With the students gone for Thanksgiving break I was primed for bird hunting. That Friday afternoon I had hunted pheasants over my Brittany, Kali, and had been getting a number of points on both hens and roosters. During my afternoon hunt, the day was marked by light to moderate winds and occasional sprinkles. Hunting pheasants in these conditions can be close to perfect, and that day, it was perfect. Mallards swirling into adjacent harvested cornfields to feed, circling and landing in nearby wetlands, and quacking incessantly also added to that days enjoyment.

Predictions were for extreme winds out of the northwest starting later in the evening and continuing all the next day (Saturday) so I knew pheasant hunting would get tough. Heavy rains were predicted during the night. In most years that much moisture that late in November would have led to a severe blizzard. On my drive home I noticed that a favorite private wetland near highway 81 and near where I had been pheasant hunting was being heavily used by mallards. With the predicted high winds reaching over 40 miles per hour from the northwest on Saturday, I decided to concentrate on ducks the next morning. After getting permission from the landowner, I called Carter

Johnson to see if he was free to set up for ducks on this wetland—I knew his answer before I asked. For Carter, duck hunting, duck cooking, and duck eating are critical and essential parts of life during any fall. Carter Johnson is a long-time hunting companion that was on the faculty with me at SDSU.

That night the heavy rains came in classic South Dakota style. We arrived near the wetland a little after sunrise the next morning hoping that many of the ducks on the wetland would already be out field feeding. The rain had stopped but the wind had an icy feel and bit hard on our uncovered faces. We put on our cold waders and warmed up by hiking about 200 yards to the wetland, flushing hundreds of ducks as we approached. Almost all of these late season ducks were mallards. Many of these ducks set back into the wetland in the high winds.

There was dense cattail and river bulrush cover around the edges of the approximately eight to ten-acre wetland so we began to set out decoys but quickly found that the steady high winds and extreme gusts were tossing and tipping the decoys like tiny toys even in the most wind-protected spots. Peak winds easily exceeded 40 miles per hour and the steady wind seemed almost as bad.

After a few minutes we decided it was impossible to use the decoys in this howling north wind. We hatched a new plan. We hid with our dogs in the downwind edge of cattails and started hunting. Hundreds of ducks on the water upwind from us acted as decoys and apparently could not hear our shooting in the fierce wind. Multiple flocks of mallards in regular succession streamed into the wetland from the south, often flying 15 to 20 yards directly over our heads. The influence of muddy fields from the heavy rains was evident; the ducks were weighed down by mud on their feet and bill and by corn shucks sticking to their feet and trailing in the wind. Some of them looked like they were carrying yellow-gray flags as they flew low over our heads, ignoring us, looking only at the ducks already on the water. With their full gullets the mallards looked boxy and overweight toward the front—they were fully committed to getting back to the water.

There have been few times that I have seen mallards come into a wetland so steadily and rapidly. You could also see mallard flocks circling and landing in the surrounding muddy cornfields in all directions and landing in another wetland several 100 yards from us. Beautiful greenheads, fat mallards, flagged mallards, muddy-billed mallards, tasty mallards, thousands of mallards—oh what a day!

Soon it was over and we took our five drakes apiece plus a couple of Canada geese and headed home. Neither of us shall ever forget that hunt, that day, those moments, those mallards.

Unlike upland bird hunting, duck hunting in South Dakota is based on a drawing for permits in the late spring or early summer.

Ch. 60. Ice hole waterfowl, kids, and a pup

It was Saturday in early November, a little over a week after the famous Halloween blizzard (1991) that will long be remembered by folks in South Dakota and Minnesota. Following a balmy late October, this massive storm hit and caused plenty of changes in plans for everyone, including hunters. A fair number of pheasants were caught in marginal cover and some of those did not make it through the storm. Waterfowl migrated in mass ahead of the storm and some weathered those conditions on larger lakes that still had spots with open water. With deep drifts of snow it was difficult or impossible to travel for a few days. We were still able to hunt pheasants, mostly in the cattail sloughs where many had concentrated.

I had arranged to take my son Ryan on a hunting trip with his high school buddy, Jonathan Jenks, Jr., whose father, Jon, happened to be my favorite deer hunting companion. Ryan was mostly into computers but he could be enticed into a hunt, especially if Jonathan joined us and if we did not leave early in the morning. I brought hot chocolate, lunches, and plenty of other goodies for eating to keep the troops happy. Our plans were to hunt waterfowl in the morning if we could find an open water spot near shore (and hiding cover) on a water body and then to chase pheasants in the afternoon. For pheasant hunting, we brought along Connie Gates Brittany pup, Lindy, that I had trained after my Brittany Rascal was killed by a vehicle. Lindy was less than nine months old but was already proficient at pointing pheasants and retrieving, despite my concern about her getting spurred. Lindy became a fabulous pheasant dog and I regularly borrowed her from Connie for hunts until she pointed and retrieved her last birds at 13 years.

We drove over a ridge northwest of Lake Preston and there on an unfamiliar body of water (about 300 acres) was a massive flock of lesser snow geese, Canada geese, and ducks, in or surrounding a small ice hole no more than 70 yards wide and extending 30 yards out into the lake. The ice hole was nicely located at the tip of a small rocky, brushy point. We found the landowner and got permission to hunt waterfowl and pheasants on his land. We then flushed the waterfowl using the open water area. The near shore ice was thick enough to cautiously walk on so we placed about two dozen Canada goose shells and a few mallard decoys on the ice so they looked like they were resting near the open water. The Canada goose shells looked especially enticing. It was a perfect setup for a couple of kids in their mid teens.

My son Ryan and his friend Jonathan Jenks Jr. (right) set up for our perfect ice-hole waterfowl hunt.

Before we could check the water depth (it looked deep to me) Lindy walked around the ice hole to the far side and promptly fell into a slushy mixture of ice chunks. She could not get back on the ice and seemed bound by the slush. The ice edge near her looked too thin and dangerous for approaching her from that side. I thought of how I would tell Connie if I could not get her puppy out of the floating matt of slush and back on top of the ice in time. Brittanys were never built for swimming very long in icy waters. What if Lindy died right there! How long could she last in the ice slush before going under? Do I take a swim to get her out or will I go down in the attempt? What should I do? I decided to see if I could call her out of the slush over toward the edge of the ice hole closer to shore where there was no slush and where I could grab her collar or paw and pull her out. It seemed to take forever (several minutes) for her to get out of the slush but the idea worked. For a few minutes I thought I had saved the dog from drowning.

After this harrowing experience I decided we needed to get some depths on the ice hole so I found a willow limb to check the depth of the "deep" water. You guessed it! The murky water was less than two feet deep nearest the ice edge closest to shore. I then used my chest waders to wade across the ice hole to the floating slush mixture and found it was less than three feet at the deepest. Still, it was pretty rewarding for a few minutes thinking I had saved the dog. Such quick thinking in such a "dangerous" situation!

Sometimes my thinking seems to follow along similar lines to this "ice hole emergency" on many important issues. That is, I fail to size up the entire situation and the magnitude of the challenge until somewhere midway through the experience or even after the experience is nearly over. Sometimes I don't get the picture until years later. That probably applies to most people and to all kinds of things in life like marriage, rearing children, scientific research, going to college, or even to countries getting into costly and deadly wars. Napoleon found this out after charging deep into Russia, victoriously reaching Moscow, and then caught by the deadly winter, losing all as he tried to back track the 500 miles to safety.

Oh yes, it was a dream hunt for the kids with ducks and geese regularly coming back to land in the ice hole. Our mostly natural blind provided good concealment and a small fire kept the kids warm. Both Ryan and Jonathan made some nice shots on swinging ducks, Canada geese, and snow geese. I had the kids help pluck our bounty and then found out too late after looking at some wing feathers that Ryan had shot a greater scaup that I needed for the bird collection at SDSU.

No, giant Canada geese don't average 15 to16 pounds as too many published hunting stories tell you. Still, they are plenty big and once in a while you will break the 14-pound mark. Hunters really do tend to stretch the truth on those trophies. We finished the day chasing after some of the pheasants that had been crowing at us during the duck hunt. South Dakota, what a place to be!

Jonathan Jenks, Jr. (left) and my son Ryan after the ice-hole waterfowl hunt. Plenty of work left plucking these ducks and geese.

Ch. 61. Whitetails, pheasants, and more

It is around 2 a.m. and I'm unable to get back to sleep. My worst enemy for getting enough sleep is when I start thinking about favorite memories or new ideas. So here I am thinking about South Dakota again and memories from deer and pheasant hunting in McPherson County north of Eureka. Jon Jenks and I usually made an annual trip to hunt deer in mid November at this north-central South Dakota site. Jon has conducted plenty of research on whitetails and other large ungulates and has published much of this work in scientific journals. But this is not a research trip and this internationally recognized researcher gets no special considerations or respect from the deer, pheasants, or me on this hunting trip. Jon is a good buddy and we have a great time visiting on this trip or any other time we get a chance. We also seem to share a common sense of humor in our conversations so the dialogue gets pretty interesting. I definitely miss having Jon Jenks around since moving to Utah.

Hunters can get plenty of deer licenses in South Dakota including multiple antlerless licenses with a bow and a rifle permit. Hunters can also purchase leftover licenses and can often get more than one buck license if they are willing to travel around the state. White-tailed deer are common throughout most of the state while mule deer are most common in parts of western South Dakota. East River archery and rifle permits, West River permits, national wildlife refuge permits, and Black Hills permits—a great place if you like to deer hunt! In Utah where I now live, you get basically one bow permit or one rifle permit for taking a buck mule deer in the general season. You cannot have both. Except in limited hunts you cannot take antlerless deer. While Utah has some impressive trophy mule deer, deer hunting opportunities in South Dakota for residents and even nonresidents are much more available. South Dakota has the most incredible hunting opportunities!

A couple of times on grouse and pheasant hunts in western South Dakota, getting back to our lodging in the post sunset period has been made challenging and a bit dangerous because of the numbers of deer crossing the highway. Unbelievable numbers of white-tailed deer build up in some years but then a viral disease strikes sooner or later and the numbers decline. When about 60% of the fawns are getting pregnant in the fall (at 6 months) and the yearling and older does are dropping twins regularly, white-tailed deer numbers can get out of hand pretty fast.

Now, to get back to my story. One complication for me on deer hunts was being distracted by pheasants and prairie grouse since I would rather hunt upland birds over a dog than go after deer. The area we were hunting had pheasants and sharptails plus an occasional flock of gray partridge so I made sure to bring the hunting dog on the trip. The primary place we hunted was a farm-ranch operation covering a few thousand acres and owned by a friend that had been a student in a couple of my classes' years earlier. Mark had graduated with a BS degree in Wildlife and Fisheries Sciences. He was an excellent student and worked well with people so he soon found career opportunities with the U.S. Fish and Wildlife Service. However, after several years he had the opportunity to take over the family farm in McPherson County. He has been farming and ranching since and he has a wonderful wildlife area all his own. We also had permission to hunt some other adjacent land in the area.

On this particular morning I posted the end of a shelterbelt that featured a heavily used deer trail. Jon had posted a spot on a different section of land. The section I chose had extensive cover in the form of tall grasses and forbs and several wetlands. The area was enrolled in the Conservation Reserve Program. The distractions that morning caused primarily by ring-necked pheasants were nothing short of ridiculous although the 10 a.m. start time for pheasants made it easier to stick with the deer hunt. In the early light of morning the chances of getting a whitetail were considerable and the cacophony caused by cackling and crowing rooster pheasants was especially impressive. There were cock pheasants jumping into the air in their frequent jousting contests, pheasants landing nearby, and pheasants walking within my view. In the midst of this I could hear sharp-tailed grouse dancing on a traditional lek, probably on a knoll or hill with short grass, as they often do in both the fall and the spring. Spring dancing by these grouse is much more intensive. A year earlier, in a nearby spot, several sharptails landed in the small tree that I was using as cover near a major deer trail. I was less than six feet from the closest grouse and learned some grouse language new to me. Very talkative little guys!

As I am listening to and watching these upland game birds plus other small birds like black-capped chickadees and dark-eyed juncos in the trees and shrubs around me, I am suddenly brought to attention by the sight of antlers and ears approaching through the tall grass. The buck walks right at me to about 25 yards and stops. Something is amiss ahead of him but, even though I am shaking badly, it is too late for this buck. The 5 x 5 looks to be a three-year old from tooth wear and the antlers are fairly impressive. I'm not really out to break trophy records and I'm plenty happy filling my tag with this nice buck. For me it is a trophy. I gut the buck, keeping the liver and heart, and drag him to a nearby trail where I can bring my truck. Before noon I fill my doe tag and my family is pretty well set with corn-fed deer for the year. I'm thinking I should have purchased an additional doe tag. Jon has probably scored too on deer but I won't see him until lunch. Now I can get after those pheasants and maybe some grouse this afternoon.

Ch. 62. A campfire visit from a Charles Manson look-alike

It was April in the early 2000s and I was camped at a mostly empty public campground a little west of Hot Springs South Dakota. I had been hunting Merriam's turkeys in the ponderosa pine landscape of the southern Black Hills and had shot a nice gobbler. I set up my tent and was enjoying the evening sitting by a warm campfire. In the midst of this enjoyable moment a banged up old vehicle and a younger couple arrived and set up a tent about 50 yards from me. About the time I was ready to get some sleep, the man from this nearby campsite walked up and sat down by the fire. He introduced himself and started doing a lot of talking—he was intoxicated. The man had a dark beard and looked to be in his early 30s. I was amazed how much he looked like pictures I had seen of Charles Manson, the mass murderer, in the flickering light of the campfire. It was an eerie feeling! He started telling me about his life and about his girlfriend. He obviously had had plenty of different jobs but did not stick with them.

At that point I noticed my dog had disappeared so I began calling her. When she got back I scolded her for taking off and this Charles Manson look-alike told me he was displeased with me for talking to my dog in that tone. He became scarily bossy about everything from the dog to putting wood on the fire. He also looked at the gobbler I had shot and told me that he had lived in the Black Hills for many years and that this gobbler was smaller than most hens. I had conducted research with graduate students in the Black Hills and I knew the range of weights for hens and toms (it was a big adult tom) but still I didn't want to argue too much with this scary guy. He told me he often shot hens and gobblers and did not need a hunting season or a license to do so. He ranted on about his dislike for any kind of authority and especially for law enforcement. Then he seemed to realize that I had told him I worked in the Wildlife and Fisheries Sciences Department at SDSU and that I might report him for killing turkeys out of season. He asked me a few questions on my intentions and I just tried to laugh it off. To allay his fears that I would report him I told him we all break the law a little here and there and that there were too many wild turkeys anyway. Since he looked like the well-known serial killer, I mainly just listened.

Sophia E Shaw

He remained at my camp for almost two hours despite my efforts to tell him it was time to get some sleep. Apparently, he figured we had become good friends. In fact, he told me to stay around until he got up in the morning so we could talk further and so he could get my address. It sounded too much like an order. I just agreed and I told him I would see him in the morning. The guy was probably harmless. Nevertheless, after he left, I loaded my shotgun and kept it beside me in my tent, hoping I could sleep safely without someone returning to attack with a hatchet or some such weapon. After all, I did have information about his frequent poaching. Seems strange now, but he just looked so much like the famous murderer. I made sure to get up at about 4:30 a.m., quietly took down my tent, and loaded the car. I kept thinking "Charles" would suddenly appear again and I was plenty glad to drive out of that campground and head for home.

Ch. 63. Camping with the mayor's permission

There are usually plenty of state camping areas in South Dakota. Hunters and anglers can also camp on most National Grassland (U.S. Forest Service), Bureau of Land Management, or Bureau of Reclamation lands although you need to check on fire laws on these federal lands. In many cases you cannot have an open fire unless it is in a regular campground. The Corp of Engineers has some great camping areas near the Missouri River. I have camped and have friends that have camped many times on these public lands during the grouse or pheasant seasons.

Gary Peterson and I had gone up to Lake Cochrane in eastern South Dakota to fly fish for bass and bluegills the day before the early September Canada goose opener. We were going to camp out that night and hunt geese the next day. The fishing was excellent but we found that the campground at Lake Cochrane was already full. We decided to try to find another place. We stopped for dinner in the tiny town of Toronto at a small café. We had noticed a city park with plenty of space so we asked the waitress (plus cook and owner) if she knew whom we could ask about possibly camping in that park. She told us that we could put up our tent and stay there for the night and that she would inform the mayor, her husband, when she got home from work. In these small towns you can really get to the heart of things with just a question or two. These are some of the best people in the world. I remember that fishing and hunting trip more for the small town camping with the mayor and mayor's wife's permission than for the fishing or hunting.

Ch. 64. Can pheasants swim?

My seven grandchildren were having a get together and swimming pool party in my daughter Margo's backyard pool in Granite Bay, California, and asked me if chickens can swim. In my mind I pictured still lively ring-necked pheasants that I had knocked down in the open water in South Dakota's many wetlands. The children were pretty surprised when I told them to pick up one of the six pet chickens and research the topic themselves—they were soon tossing more than one pet chicken into the pool. Of course the chickens floated nicely and used their wings to propel across the water and get out of the pool. My daughter came out to scold the children and grandpa for tossing chickens in the pool but she soon joined in the party. Like the chickens, pheasants float and can use their wings to propel themselves in deeper water but likely only do so in an emergency situation.

Ring-necked pheasants are highly attracted to the taller grass, forbs, and emergent vegetation in dry wetlands as well as those with standing water. Some of the dense emergent vegetation is in water too deep for pheasants to wade easily and is not normally used until ice forms to support their weight. Pheasants will certainly wade out into emergent cover into several inches of water to escape danger. At times I have surmised they must have been using the roots and tangles of emergent vegetation for support to move a little farther out into deeper water to escape hunting dogs and hunters. Sometimes birds end up flushing from wetland and emergent vegetation well beyond the water-shoreline interface and, in some cases those were in water that went over the top of my hiking boots. Pheasants won't shy from getting fairly wet on the belly if necessary for survival.

I've shot many cock pheasants that flushed from emergent vegetation in wetlands and, before ice up, a good number splashed down in water of various depths. On a few hunts where I primarily hunted wetland edges, virtually every downed pheasant splashed into the water. Not too nice for photos! Some of these wetlands were only knee deep but water in others was over my head. If your dog can see or smell the bird you are in good shape on the retrieve—fortunately that is the case in most situations. However, you might want to keep your chest waders or at least hip waders in the vehicle to avoid getting wet and cold yourself trying to retrieve a pheasant in a situation where the dog is confused by birds downed in deeper water beyond the dense and tall emergent cover. Most of the time your dog can retrieve the bird but at times I have needed waders to at least lead my dog out beyond the dense cattails so she could see or smell the downed pheasant. If you have a good retrieving dog like a Labrador this may not be a problem but remember, in this situation the dog often cannot see hand signals. I have even watched some Labrador retrievers get totally confused about the retrieve when hunting companions shot pheasants that fell out of the dogs view behind dense and wide stands of cattail cover. Oh yes, it does work fairly well to strip down and retrieve birds yourself in a secluded spot but it can be a bit cold. I have tried it a couple of times.

Pheasants will readily wade into the emergent vegetation and shallow water to escape hunters. (Courtesy of Bob Hodorff)

Ch. 65. Holding tight!

Sometime in the early 1980s, Ron Fesler moved his family from Missouri to Brooking South Dakota. Ron had never hunted pheasants so I took him out with my Brittany and he was soon hooked. Since then he has either had a Brittany or a Labrador and has been a serious pheasant hunter. On a warm day in early November in the early 1990s, Ron and I were hunting on private land that he had lined up about six miles northwest of Volga. The area was enrolled in the Conservation Reserve Program and the excellent cover had good numbers of pheasants. We had started hunting about three hours before sundown and I had filled out with three roosters. While Ron was working on his last bird I walked back to the vehicle. As I sat on the rear tailgate of his truck my dog kept hunting the nearby cover. She was working along the old road less than 15 yards from me when she locked up on a rigid point. I walked over to see if I could actually see the pheasant in the road ditch and, surprisingly, spotted the tail feathers of a cock and a bit of the colorful neck and back plumage. For some stupid reason I wanted to see if I could tickle a pheasant on the sides under the wing and that is what I did. Tickle, tickle, gotcha and have a nice day! Wow, that bird burst out of there in beautiful form, unscathed by its close call with a dangerous predator—me.

Until they moved to Idaho in 2013, I almost always stayed with Ron and Tina Fesler when I visited Brookings from my home in Utah. We have remained long-time friends. I had lots of fun kidding Ron's aging mother who lived with them. She was quite a pretty older lady and I would make sure to tell her she was still good looking and that I thought she was hot stuff. She loved the kidding but she has now passed on.

Several times I have approached a dog on point and detected the tail of a rooster and sometimes of a hen protruding from the cover. I think the long tail on roosters is a little more likely to give them away than is the somewhat shorter tail of hens. In most cases I have simply used a nudge from my boot to get the bird to fly although sometimes such birds can turn out to be pheasants that were injured when shot earlier but were never retrieved. I always try hard to capture these injured birds and add them to my daily bag—most are still edible. In a few cases I have had healthy pheasants hold so tight that I had to dig out the grass with my hands before they would finally flush. They can especially hold tight if there is a cover of snow over the vegetation with space for pheasants underneath. I discuss that further in the chapter on *A freshly fallen snow.* My Brittanys were all trained not to grab at a tight-holding pheasant unless I ordered them to fetch a downed bird. In 41 years of hunting in South Dakota with a Brittany, my dogs have incidentally captured hens no more than a couple of times. Unfortunately, I have heard reports on some flushing dogs that regularly capture and sometimes kill hens in snowy conditions. Hopefully your dog seldom captures hens or is soft mouthed enough not to hurt them.

Tying trout flies with my friend Ron Fesler (left) on a trip to Montana in August 1990. We've hunted plenty of pheasants together over the past 30 years.

Ch. 66. A nap to stay the distance

I love to hunt and sometimes that overcomes my common sense. As a senior citizen and with some arthritis in my knees I was hunting near Pierre on a windy day and found myself getting extremely tired after about five hours of hard walking. I had taken one rooster and a prairie chicken to that point. Still, I did not want to quit with the all-important preroosting hours coming. Since I had driven all the way from Utah for a couple of weeks of hunting pheasants and prairie grouse, I did not want to miss any hunting time. To remedy the problem, I took a nap in the grass near my vehicle in a warm looking spot to see how I felt when I woke up. Unlike Alaska fly fishing trips, you do not need to worry about a large brown bear coming over to check you out while you are asleep. After a half-hour nap the knees and body were ready to hunt the final hour and a half of the day, a most productive time. The nap revived me, made the remainder of the day more enjoyable, and put me into one more rooster and a flock of greater prairie-chickens before the sun set. Hunters also shoot more accurately if they are not dead tired.

My friend Gary Peterson reminds me that sometimes when we were younger (and living in South Dakota) we used to hunt ducks Saturday morning, take a short nap, and then hunt pheasants in the afternoon, often going from before sunrise to sunset. That reminds me of one of my longer and most exhausting days of bird hunting that, looking back, had a somewhat comical ending. I recall one Saturday in the 1980s when Chuck Dieter (my former graduate student and now a professor at SDSU), Dale Gates, and I hunted ducks all morning in Deuel County north of Brookings and then drove an hour to an area south of Brookings to hunt pheasants all afternoon. We were getting plenty tired by midafternoon but adrenaline spurred us on to keep hunting. At sunset Dale was bringing his 4-wheel drive pickup down the road to where Chuck and I were waiting. There was a large mud hole in the road and Dale ignored it since he had a 4-wheel drive. You can guess what happened! A half hour later with it starting to get dark and with temperatures plummeting we knew we could not get the truck out of the mud hole. This was an unusually isolated spot southwest of Brookings and three very tired hunters started hiking for a hopefully occupied farm house about two miles distant. At least the walking kept us warm. About 40 minutes later we reached the farmhouse and a helpful farmer that brought his tractor over and pulled us out. That day fits into my definition of getting too tired—a day when a midday nap would have made a big difference.

I'm still crazy enough to try early duck hunting and afternoon pheasants in the same day as long as I can crash in some soft vegetation or in the vehicle for an hour or so of sleep about midday. As for the arthritic knees I mentioned, hiking four miles per day and specific knee exercises have actually improved the situation. At least for now, I can keep chasing pheasants and avoid knee replacement surgery.

Ch. 67. Stocked pheasants—they needed wild mothers to teach them

Most of us are hopeful that our parents were not really wild in the sense that humans use the term—well maybe just a little wild. However, wild means something else in pheasants. Research has clearly shown that much of the wildness in young pheasants is learned from their wild mothers. Because of this lack of wildness in pen-reared birds, almost every avid pheasant hunter greatly prefers to hunt birds hatched in the wild and reared by a wild hen. I borrowed the catchy and accurate phrase that "pen-reared pheasants needed wild mothers to teach them" from Tony Leif, a good friend, former student, and Director of the South Dakota Department of Game, Fish and Parks Wildlife Division. I think it is a very accurate statement.

You will seldom run into stocked birds when hunting private or public lands in South Dakota unless you hunt on commercial areas and, in some cases, even commercial areas have a good supply of wild birds if they have extensive nesting habitat. The economics of releasing pheasants favors releasing full-sized roosters before the gun but the cost of this approach limits its use to commercial hunting areas where hunters pay big bucks to hunt. Many of these birds are nice looking birds and enjoyable to hunt but I still prefer hunting wild birds if given the choice. The challenge of the hunt is in the craftiness and wildness of the birds—wild-hatched birds win that contest easily. For those of you hunting released birds, I do agree that released birds can get pretty crafty if fortunate enough to survive in the wild for a few months. Of course, full sized roosters released for hunting are meant to be harvested right away in order to recover the investment.

When pheasant numbers are low the public often demands a quick answer through release of stocked birds. Survival of the traditional seven to 10-week old chicks after hatching tends to be particularly poor since they were not reared by wild hens in the wild. They simply have not learned how to avoid or even recognize predators and to survive on their own and are especially vulnerable in the first month after release. Even spring released hens have poor survival and the production of young from these pen-reared hens is much less than from an equal number of wild hens (See *Ring-necked Pheasants: Thriving in South Dakota*, Chapter 11).

Another concern with introducing large numbers of pen reared birds is the possible dilution of the genetics in wild populations. Genetic traits can affect wildness, size, flight ability, and other characteristics that are valuable in assuring the success of wild pheasant populations into the future. Released pen-reared pheasants can also introduce diseases into wild populations. These are concerns biologists have expressed about extensive releases of pen-reared pheasants. However, it should be noted that South Dakota's pheasant population descended from numerous releases of both wild and pen-reared pheasants in the early 1900s. It is likely that the releases of wild birds were much more successful than of pen-reared birds but under those ideal habitat conditions, some of the pen-reared birds must have also survived and added their genetics to the original population. (*See Ring-necked Pheasants: Thriving in South Dakota*, Chapter 1).

The best protection for wild pheasant genetics may be the poor survival of released birds since few survive to reproduce. Also, the pen-reared birds with the poorest genetic qualities for surviving in the wild would seemingly be less likely to survive and reproduce. Based on the strong response of wild pheasant populations to the recent Conservation Reserve Program, I suggest that the genetics of South Dakota's pheasant populations are still in very good shape. Unfortunately, the same cannot be said for quality pheasant habitat in many portions of the state. Give me plenty of quality nesting habitat and wintering cover and the resulting wild pheasants any day of the year over artificial release situations. Wild hatched and wild reared pheasants are what you can expect to find unless you are on or very near commercial pheasant preserves. Even some of the larger pheasant preserves with extensive habitat produce lots of wild hatched pheasants.

Ch. 68. Distinguished guests and paradise

Over the 31 years I lived in South Dakota and taught at South Dakota State University (SDSU) I often took guest speakers on pheasant hunts. Our guest speakers visited the university speaking to students and faculty. Bringing in guest speakers for students and faculty was important in developing working relationships with faculty in other universities and was valuable for our undergraduate and graduate students. It was part of our outreach program. In other words, it was a great way to get out of our own shells and to expand our thinking.

Not surprisingly, it was easiest to entice outside speakers to visit our campus during the fall hunting seasons for pheasants and waterfowl. South Dakota's reputation for bird hunting was a great asset in that regard. For some of our invited guests, it also became sort of a trap because once they had visited and hunted South Dakota they just had to come back again. In fact, they often made return trips to speak in our classes and seminars with little or no travel reimbursement. That alone attests to how good the bird hunting can be.

All of the guest speakers mentioned here completed Ph.D. degrees early in their careers and have followed with outstanding accomplishments and publications. However, most ask that I not refer to them formally as Dr. in this book. A suggestion a couple of these guests made to me was that I simply refer to them as something like "old hunters put out to pasture, spending their time kicking deer pellets or cow pies." These deer-pellet kickers are some pretty special and talented guys and they are all my good friends.

One of our regular guests was Leigh Fredrickson, a professor at the University of Missouri and the Director of the Gaylord Memorial Laboratory, a center for extensive wetland and waterfowl research. Leigh had even spent time in Antarctica working on Adelie penguins early in his career. Leigh came back many times over the three decades I was on the faculty, often

Finding Paradise in South Dakota

speaking to our students and always getting in some pheasant and duck hunting. Sometimes Leigh would even spell me in the foursome card games (rook or hearts) with Ruel and Beth (my in-laws) and Marcia at my house so I could go back to campus in the evening and get ready for the next day's lectures. Working evenings was sometimes the price I paid for hunting too much but it was worth it. I'm positive Leigh would call South Dakota a paradise. In fact, later in his career, Leigh was put on the graduate faculty at SDSU and even had students getting their masters and Ph.D. degrees at SDSU with Leigh as the major professor. Thus, the university, Leigh Fredrickson, and Gaylord Memorial Laboratory became linked together because of some early visits, friendships, and bird hunts. Since I retired in 2003 I have met Leigh almost every year for pheasant and duck hunting and for a stay at our friend Carter Johnson's hunting and fishing cabin on Lake Preston.

Leigh Fredrickson (Photo from 2012) lives in Missouri but his love for South Dakota, the people, the wetlands, and the wildlife runs especially deep.

Leigh has the perfect attitude about hunts. We have gone on plenty of pheasant hunts and I don't think it matters too much to Leigh if we get birds or not. He just has a great time watching the dog work and being out hunting. Some days we put up lots of roosters, sometimes very few, but Leigh is never disappointed. I can say the same thing for our waterfowl hunts. I'm always sure we had a great hunt if Leigh came along but it was especially a great one if we saw thousands of waterfowl in the air even if we didn't get close to one of them. One afternoon we set up goose decoys in a field near Carter's cabin in an attempt to decoy field feeding waterfowl. No geese came by but mallards and pintails by the thousands circled the field late in the day coming within about 50 yards. The ducks were too far out to shoot at without risking wounding birds but they were especially fun to watch as they swerved about the field in huge tight flocks. I don't think we shot or shot at a single bird that evening. Leigh just loves to be in the field and to see all those wild birds in wild places and that is the way I wish all hunters felt.

Wildlife research biologists often need to capture grouse and other wild species to mark them with radio transmitters or obtain other data. Jack Connelly completed his Ph.D. working on greater sage-grouse out of my alma mater (Washington State University) and has continued to work on sage grouse and other grouse through his career. Jack captured and marked plenty of grouse over many years as principal wildlife research biologist with the Idaho Department of Fish and Game until his recent retirement. As an internationally recognized grouse specialist, you would think he would be pretty smart but I set a trap for Jack and caught him easily. That trap was simply to invite him to SDSU to speak to our students and faculty. We snared this biologist right away and he returned to South Dakota to speak to students and faculty and hunt pheasants with me for many years. In fact, I still often meet him there for fall hunts. Jack has vouched for how terrific the upland bird hunting can be in South Dakota with his annual trips to the state. Living in scenic Idaho, Jack has some pretty good pheasant and grouse hunting at home but not as great as South Dakota offers.

Jack Connelly in one of his secret pheasant and grouse spots in central South Dakota in 2012. Actually his secret spot can be pretty slow in some years.

For those thinking about visiting South Dakota, Jack Connelly can especially attest to how friendly the small town folks and landowners can be. Try any small town café for a few days and the local folks will be looking for you at breakfast and dinner. Some folks will even be waiting for your arrival in ensuing years if you go back more than a couple of times. You tend to make friends and contacts when you hunt an area on a regular basis. Jack and his regular hunting companion, Doug Finicle, really know how to make friends since Doug brings bags of fresh Idaho spuds to give out. These guys bring two German shorthairs (Jack's dogs) and two Brittany spaniels (Doug's dogs) so they are well prepared for the hunt. In 2010 Jack tore his Achilles tendon on a Idaho bird hunt when he stepped in a badger hole not long before the planned South Dakota trip. He could not make the trip to Idaho so Doug Finicle and I hunted without him but, on Jack's request (which he denies), called him each day or twice per day to give him updates on the hunting

Finding Paradise in South Dakota

action. We of course talked up each days exciting hunts but did not allow Jack to bemoan or cry about the situation. Be careful of those badger holes! These guys are extremely secretive about the spots they hunt, even if those spots are not that good some years.

The late Dr. Jim Teer, Director of the Rob and Bessie Welder Wildlife Foundation in south Texas and Distinguished Professor Emeritus at Texas A&M University, also visited our Department and was able to spend a couple of days pheasant hunting. I was successful in putting him on a good number of Brittany points on ring-necked pheasants. I remember Jim saying to me to my best recollection "Les, you don't realize what you have here. This is a wildlife and hunting wonderland." Jim Teer had traveled as a wildlife consultant on several continents and seen wildlife and habitats beyond anything I will likely see in my lifetime. It left me with a strong impression when Jim described South Dakota as a wonderland.

Dr. Teer was instrumental in bringing my graduate student, Mini Nagendran, to the Welder Wildlife Refuge where she completed her research for an M.S. degree. Mini was from India and knew English better than most students native to the United States or Canada, probably because her mother was an English teacher. After graduating from SDSU Mini went on to complete her Ph.D. and become a specialist on cranes. She also added a doctorate degree in veterinary medicine. Her accomplishments and career were greatly influenced by Jim Teer. I still remember going with Mini to catch channel catfish and to check the crab traps in the Aransas River on the Welder Wildlife Refuge. We needed the fish and crabs for a dinner celebration. While we were fishing and visiting along the river bank our flashlights revealed the bright reflections from the eyes of a large alligator approaching us. The alligator probably just wanted some fish but you should have seen how quickly we moved up the steep bank. I still hear from Mini and her husband Jim each year.

It was fun to have Jerran Flinders visit as a guest speaker from Brigham Young University where he had conducted research and published on a wide variety of mammals from black-tailed jackrabbits, to elk, and mountain lions. I knew Jerran was an excellent teacher and that his research background would make for an interesting talk for our students and faculty. Jerran is one of my long-time friends that I had met when we were both working on our dissertation research out of Fort Collins, Colorado. We had young families at that time. We have memories of chasing a few monstrous mule deer in dense fog and fly fishing for trout on favorite rivers like the Poudre. We can tell you that dense fog can ruin chances for tagging even one of the five well scouted trophy bucks in a secret canyon. You could barely see 30 feet that opening morning! Neither of us will forget the night when war radicals (about 1970) burned down a campus buildings next to where we had research offices at Colorado State University. Though I was in Fort Collins, I was still a graduate student at Washington State University. Jerran's visit to SDSU coincided with a poor pheasant year in eastern South Dakota but we still coupled the visit with some pheasant hunting. I even apologized for the poor bird numbers before the hunt started. Forget that! On our first days hunt my Brittany proceeded to point over 12 roosters in good shooting range. It took that many flushed roosters for us to get our limit of those magnificent birds. I remember Jerran remarking that for a down year in pheasant numbers it looked like awfully good hunting to him. We were a bit lucky in getting that many birds up that day but poor pheasant years in South Dakota are usually better than good years in most other states.

Several other wildlife and fisheries professors and specialists from other universities were also brought in as guest speakers, usually during the fall. Most of these guests left with memories and stories to share about pheasants, waterfowl, and wonderful South Dakota. These guests had important implications for our department and students in numerous ways. It is fun to remember a few of the guest speakers because their appreciation for what South Dakota offered was a reminder to us of what a great place we lived in. It was and still is a great place to live or to visit.

Ch. 69. Carter's hunting cabin—a few memories

Leigh Fredrickson and I were at Carter Johnson's hunting and fishing cabin on the south side of Lake Preston, a meandered lake about 30 miles west of Brookings. We usually have a key so we can stay at the cabin as long as we want. Leigh and I had spent the last couple of hours hunting pheasants in the shoreline cover and planned to meet Carter and Martin Maca (also on the faculty at SDSU) later that day for a couple of days at the cabin. We usually spend our time duck hunting a few hundred yards from the cabin in the mornings and, in the afternoons chase after pheasants. Of the four of us, I'm the only one that has not had a heart stent performed and I'm told that family genetics and moderately high cholesterol are not in my favor. Still, none of us admit to getting old.

Carter's cabin is decorated with mounted waterfowl, pheasants, deer antlers, trophy fish, decoys, outdoor photos, and other items that make hunters and anglers feel like they have found the ultimate shelter. For some reason the wildlife mounts, the giant northern pike, the trophy white-tailed deer mounts, the waterfowl, all look especially mystic when you wander about the cabin with a flashlight in the middle of the night. Accompanied by the combined snoring (I'm sure I do my part) in the cabin, such nighttime wanderings are somewhat surreal. I think most old guys get up now and then in the night. There is a story to every wall-mounted specimen and every photo. All these species live near the cabin but the mounts come from hunts and fishing trips all over South Dakota and into Canada.

In the mornings you can always step out on the porch and hear cock pheasants crowing in the native grasses and in the wetland cover all around. The sound of ducks quacking (and whistling) and geese honking can almost always be heard except when the lake is completely frozen over. At times, as when over a hundred thousand lesser snow geese roosted in shoreline waters by the cabin, the roar of geese is all pervasive all night long.

Finding Paradise in South Dakota

There had to have been over a half million snow geese on the lake that night. I particularly like those sounds when you can clearly tell there are thousands of snow geese and other waterfowl setting their wings in the dark, high above Lake Preston, to join those already on the water or closer to landing. Fortunately, those of us who have stayed at the cabin love the sound of the geese and ducks at night. I sleep better to this kind of natural music.

Carter usually cooks up roasted duck or duck stir fry—they both taste wonderful. The aroma from cooking adds to meals as does the dinnertime conversation. A couple of times we consumed two roasted ducks each (one larger duck like a mallard and one teal) with lots of other accompanying food. Regardless of the duck species, Carter makes them irresistible eating. We usually pick the bones clean. One fall day Carter and Leigh Fredrickson (just arrived from Missouri) were sitting down to dinner in Brookings to eat a rotisserie cooked drake canvasback when I dropped in all the way from Utah. That was one good eating duck and Carter swears that I sensed the moment and timed my visit to South Dakota just to get a share of that canvasback. Pretty good senses on my part from over a thousand miles away in Utah. Okay, just lucky timing!

For the evening we have a toasty fire that lights the room through the glass stove front and we spend the hours visiting on the years happenings, memories, and other mostly light-hearted matters. We even get ideas related to our research work on wildlife, river systems, wetlands, things we need to write, and other matters. Logs are on the porch and we keep the fire stoked all evening.

I think of others who have joined us at the cabin to stay over or just to join us for dinner. Chuck Dieter, KC Jensen, Gary Peterson, Pete Schaeffer, Chuck McMullen, Steve Chipps, all faculty at SDSU and all avid hunters and fishermen. Kurt Forman with the U.S. Fish and Wildlife Service, a former student from SDSU, recently joined us because he could not resist the wildlife dinner and the company. Kurt is working hard to save South Dakotas remaining wetlands, grasslands, and wildlife. All or most are hunters, all good friends, and all enjoying the fire, the conversation, and the dinner. I have spent great days with most of these guys, working dogs, calling ducks, watching, shooting, and visiting. Carter even brings local landowners over for a wild game dinner now and then. And one night, a vagabond from the railroad a quarter mile away, broke out a window and slept the night, taking nothing of value from the cabin. But then he would have looked strange to his other railroad friends packing mounted deer head trophies, full bodied duck or goose mounts, or a huge northern pike mount.

The wildlife mounts look especially mystic when you wander about the cabin with a flashlight at night.

The two Brittanys watch all evening for any dropped snacks or other food but finally settle in and doze in a corner. Food, warmth from the fire, and conversation leave us all a bit sleepy after a couple of hours. About this time I climb the spiral staircase, climb into my sleeping bag on the bed, and soon fall asleep. I learned the hard way to be careful on the spiral stairs after I suddenly lost my balance while climbing with a sleeping bag in one hand and a day pack in the other. I did some type of reverse move on the stairs like the clumsiest gymnast, an impressive move for my age, and took a nose dive, following the rail down head first in rapid fashion. Nothing more than some substantial scrapes and a little healthy blood after the fall but it made for a loud crash and an interesting memory; the other guys like to remind me of that swan dive. The floor was undamaged. We will be up for breakfast at 5 a.m. and ready for another interesting day chasing ducks and pheasants. Anyone for hot gadwall and pheasant sandwiches for lunch?

Carter Johnson (Carter's cabin) and his Brittany, Ruby, in 2011 after a pheasant hunt. Big bluestem can be tall and dense as in this planted stand on a friends land.

Ch. 70. More hunting cabin memories, loss of a good friend

I woke up in the middle of the night in Springville filled with additional memories associated with Carter's cabin. I need to write them down. Hundreds of thousands of lesser snow geese and other waterfowl were stacked up on Lake Preston in mid November. We stayed at the cabin but made sure we arose early to get the snow goose decoys set out and ready 45 minutes before sunrise. In the darkness, accompanied by the sounds of massive numbers of snow geese still on Lake Preston, we set out our flag-type decoys in a picked cornfield where Chuck Dieter had located feeding snow geese the evening before. The site was on a moderately sloped but impressive glacial hill north of the lake. Soon, in the early dawn, we could see and hear the geese roaring into the air and heading out to feed. Huge flocks, easily visible from the glacial hill, flew our way toward their previous day's feeding site. We watched flock after flock of thousands of snow geese approaching and then spiraling from the sky into the decoys around Carter, Chuck, his son Nick, Gary Peterson, and me. All of us below those geese, close to those geese, spellbound by those geese, in the middle of the goose tornado. White phase snows, eagle heads, so many geese, so much noise, so much adrenaline, and later, so much work cleaning geese.

Chuck Dieter knows how to hunt geese. During this hunt I was calling hard on my snow goose call and noticed Chuck was not calling at all. He knew that thousands of snow geese drown out the meager calls from hunters. Taking a lesson from Chuck, I stopped trying to call when there were thousands of geese in the air and saved my voice. To others that hunt snow geese all the time, such hunts may not be memorable but for me it was memorable. For me it makes a nice memory of South Dakota, or at least so it seemed when I awoke in the middle of this particular night.

In November in the 1990s I vividly recall finding a picked cornfield 10 miles south of Carter's cabin filled with mallards and snow geese. Luckily, I knew the owner. I obtained permission to hunt and would take Carter, and two other good friends from my department, Mike Brown and Dave Willis, to this field the next morning. I remember standing by my truck at Carter's cabin in the 5 a.m. darkness with my flashlight and watching two striped skunks run two yards behind me along the vehicle trail just as Mike and Dave drove up to Carter's cabin from Brookings for the hunt. If I recall, they saw the skunks and inadvertently chased them ahead of their vehicle to my feet. Glad I did not step backwards!

Now, getting back to the images I still have of that day's hunt. Thousands of migrating mallards setting their wings for our decoys and the picked cornfield from great heights, low-flying lesser snow geese coming to the decoys, a few white-fronted geese hanging just above us, the brisk wind buffeting the birds, and periodic flurries of snow melting as the crystals touched the earth—so many great memories. It was a very successful hunt, but memories of the birds in flight, their numbers, and their nearness seem more memorable than any success in harvesting birds.

I mentioned Dave Willis in my memories of that November day just described. Dave suffered heart failure at age 58 in January 2014 while on an ice fishing trip with his wife and a grandchild. It was a huge loss and a shock for so many, for the Department of Natural Resource Management at SDSU, for the university, and especially for his wife Susie and his family. I was fortunate to hunt with Dave many times but not as often as I wish I had. I think of standing with Dave in cattail cover beside my 14-foot duck boat and having mallard flocks hanging close over the decoys at Fox Slough. I have memories of Dave, Chuck Scalet, and me in a picked cornfield with giant Canada goose decoys on the ground and giant Canada geese within 25 yards, all around us, some with their feet about to touch the ground. Of multiple hunts of migrating snow geese and large sets of rag decoys in picked cornfields and of tired, soil-smudged hunters. A great teacher, fisheries researcher, writer, and administrator (department head) crossed into the eternities. Dave's kindness, his thoughtfulness, his professionalism, will be remembered by the many whose lives he influenced for good.

Dave Willis (right) with my son Ryan on one of our goose hunts in Deuel County. This was Ryan's first Canada goose. Notice the white-fronted goose Dave is holding.

Ch. 71. Meandered lakes and changing habitats

With two roosters in hand, I had just returned from hunting in the attractive pheasant cover along the edge of Lake Preston. I had hunted the edge of the lake a mile beyond the area next to Carter's cabin and property, assuming no one would contest that it was within the meandered lake boundary. The shoreline zone was perfect for pheasants with some areas along the lake edge sporting 50 to 80 yards (width) of good cover and with harvested corn on the adjacent private uplands. Plenty of pheasants make use of the edge cover.

I include this section so hunters will be more aware of meandered lakes as possible hunting areas for pheasants and, additionally, to provide a feel for the dramatic successional changes that can occur in South Dakota wetland water levels and wetland vegetation over time. These successional changes are highly important in influencing vegetation and open water characteristics on available wetland habitat. Such changes are mostly natural and are healthy for wetlands; these changes have major influences on year-to-year use of specific wetlands by pheasants, waterfowl, white-tailed deer, and other wildlife.

Since 1972 I have watched Lake Preston change from an enormous marsh (several miles long) with interspersed patches of open, shallow water and emergent plants (like cattails and bulrushes) to an open lake (after about 1985) supporting a fair yellow perch fishery. In the shallow marsh stage, Lake Preston, in addition to attracting ducks, attracted thousands of wintering pheasants in the dense patches of emergent cover, especially where waste grain was near. That shallow marsh stage should return again in the years to come if water from drainage of smaller wetlands in the large watershed do not flood it permanently and ruin the natural successional cycle. Unfortunately, extensive drainage and ruin to the natural cycle is happening to a great extent and over a broad area. There is apparently no legal way to stop people from draining onto a neighbors land and from flooding those downstream or lower in the watershed. Over the years I even recall news reports on a couple of violent confrontations with guns over draining onto a neighbors land in eastern South Dakota. Too much or too little water can bring strong feelings!

Pheasant cover in Lake Preston was most optimal in years when water levels were lowest. In the driest years surface water was very limited and we used the zig-zag level ditching as canoe access to areas with surface water during duck season. The wetland supported a prolific array of cattails, various bulrushes, and other volunteer plants that sprout and thrive on the moist soils or grow as emergent vegetation in the shallow waters. In years that I hunted this area prior to flooding (before 1985), Lake Preston ranged from mostly dry to a classic hemimarsh (about half open water and half emergent vegetation). Being a meandered lake, public access is allowed although I was never sure of the exact legality of what was meandered and what was private near the shoreline. Neither are the court rulings clear on this. No one ever bothered me about trespass as long as I stayed in the basin or along the weedy shoreline.

Two other large meandered lakes in Kingsbury County that can provide extensive pheasant habitat and access during low water stages include Lake Thompson and Lake Whitewood. These lakes have been flooded and have been more important as fishing lakes than as pheasant winter-cover areas since 1985. There is a considerable amount of land that has been placed in public ownership near the two lakes, providing thousands of acres of upland habitat and access for hunting or fishing even during the flooded stages. Several other meandered lakes exist in East River South Dakota that hunters can check out with the Register of Deeds Office in Pierre.

Ch. 72. Hunting and staying out of trouble at home

I am convinced from research and long-term records on pheasants, pheasant habitat, and hunting season length, that pheasant season length has virtually no influence on year-to-year numbers of ring-necked pheasants. Pheasants are short-lived birds and roosters do not lay eggs nor do they assist in rearing the chicks. Lack of fertility in pheasant egg clutches has never been a problem in a pheasant population no matter how heavily the roosters have been hunted. However, at times I have wondered if divorces for avid upland game hunters increased with significant expansion in length of the pheasant season. Of course, if both spouses enjoy pheasant hunting it could also be a bonding experience.

While hunting grouse on Fort Pierre National Grassland (FPNG), Dale Gates and I met a grouse hunter (mentioned earlier) from a west coast state that brought his camper trailer and hunted grouse for several weeks every fall. In fact, he may have returned too many times for too long since he told us him and his wife had recently split up. Probably would have happened anyway but maybe the grouse hunts were a tipping point. Something for all married hunters to consider when you take long hunting trips on a regular basis. I think about Marcia since I leave her back home for almost three weeks every year while I travel to South Dakota but I'm not really worried about splitting up. Dale Gates ran into the grouse hunter from the camper trailer and his new wife recently. He had apparently remarried a gal that enjoyed accompanying him on the trip to South Dakota. You never know what will touch off marriage problems but hopefully, it will not be hunting. The wife of a professor friend of mine left him several years ago and the only negative words he could recall before she left was her telling him to "stop following her around." Sounds familiar, Marcia tells me that all the time when we go shopping together. I'm thinking that too much hunting by one spouse is probably not the root cause for very many divorces.

While I was staying at Ron and Tina Fesler's home near Brookings as I often did, another hunter and his wife were also visiting. Ron and I hunt pheasants together often and our families were also close because we attended the same small church. This visiting archery hunter was not after pheasants but instead had returned to South Dakota after having killed a trophy white-tailed deer the previous year by waiting in a tree stand near a heavily used deer trail that Ron had shown him. The archery hunter made the statement that his South Dakota deer hunt the previous year was the hunt of a lifetime. His wife seemed so supportive and I thought that it was amazing that she would travel over a thousand miles with him to stay with the Feslers for a week while her husband bow hunted. What an incredibly dedicated wife! That evening we were all playing family card games and the visiting hunter, tired from a long day and needing to head out long before dawn the next morning to get in his tree stand, went upstairs to get some sleep. His wife, after her husband had gone to bed for the night, expressed a concern that caught me by surprise. To paraphrase her statement: "I don't know how many hunts of a lifetime I can put up with anymore." They are still together.

My wife Marcia has no interest in hunting and reminds me that when we were first married (and when I thought she was still infatuated with me) I actually went chukar hunting where we lived in Washington and had her trying to push chukars toward me in a steep canyon on the Snake River. Pretty dumb move on my part but the marriage has still lasted, even though the method did not work for marriage togetherness or for chukars.

I'm sure my excessive hunting, primarily after pheasants, was a bit of a strain on our marriage when we were young and Marcia was left to care for our young children. However, I was almost always home in the evenings since good hunting was close to Brookings and I rarely hunted on the Sabbath as that was the family and church day. I probably got in the most trouble when we had a fall social event at our house on Saturday nights since I often hunted hard for ducks in the morning and pheasants in the afternoon. All-day hunting left me in pretty tough shape for socializing Saturday evenings. I fell fast asleep on the couch with our home full of guests at a few parties during those days. Marcia was a pretty good sport about it and, on my behalf, I did usually make it until about 10 p.m. before zonking out. It was a way to tell people that the party was about over although good friends sometimes stayed on anyway or just woke me up.

Taking the children on outdoor outings, including hunting, can be a real positive in keeping the family together. I did get in some family fishing trips with the children but Margo and Kim were not into hunting. They did pick up some of my interest in identifying and watching birds although they would not really admit such until they were nearly adults. My son Ryan had an interest in hunting if we brought a friend, hot chocolate, and lots of snacks. Being with Ryan when he shot his first pheasant, duck, Canada goose, and deer are all great memories. However, Ryan did not have the intense interest I have in hunting. Computers seemed to fill that role in his life and fortunately have also ended up being his ticket to a career in information technology, a field in which he excels and greatly enjoys

Today Marcia seems to appreciate that I stay active and out of the rocking chair by hunting, and other outdoor activities. A few of our friends have even asked us how to get their retired spouse active with activities like fly fishing, and hiking so they will get out of the house and get some exercise. Marcia is quite independent and takes trips of her own with old friends, including traveling with friends she taught with in her many years at Brooking High School, gatherings with her old high school sorority friends (the Slugs) at cabin sites on Washington's coastal beaches near Aberdeen, and trips to places like New York City. Glad I could skip the New York City trip! Marcia and I also go on joint vacations, especially to snorkel in warm ocean waters and to see our children and grandchildren. After 48 years of marriage we are still married and we are still friends. Oh yes, dinner out every week and flowers also help.

Ch. 73. Loose feathers, spurs, and processed game birds

There are plenty of differences of opinion on whether to hang game birds for aging or process them right away. Two friends visiting Brookings from out of state in early November kept their week's kill of pheasants uncleaned (entrails left inside bird) and hung from the neck on a wire line set up in my garage; that method for aging the meat seemed to work fine in early November. I think some of my neighbors that spotted that long line of hanging birds wondered if I had taken far more than my legal limit. Those that hang pheasants or other birds to age the meat claim the process improves the unique taste of wild birds and tenderizes mature birds. Aging birds is popular in many cultures and has plenty of supporters so I suspect it has some important values for influencing taste and tenderness, especially in adult birds. I think I need to heed the wisdom of these several cultures and try this carcass aging process further.

However you care for the harvested birds, be sure to leave the leg (spur), wing, or head attached so they are legal for transportation from the field to your home. During the early grouse season and even into the early weeks of pheasant season, taking along a cooler with ice can be a good idea for keeping harvested birds out of the heat. It is not unusual for the temperature to reach over 70 degrees Fahrenheit in the early pheasant season. In the 2003 general opener for pheasants, temperatures were in the 80s and even into the 90s in some areas of South Dakota. Pretty hot for the third weekend in October. Such temperatures are even more common a month earlier during the grouse opener.

I usually process game birds on the same day I shoot them. I like to leave the spur on packaged pheasants so I can decide if it is an old or young bird for culinary purposes. Plenty of hunters incorrectly call older juvenile pheasants adults so you might want to be careful on that account. I sometimes probe the bursa of Fabricius (see pg. 23. *Ring-Necked Pheasants: Thriving in South Dakota*) with the base of a flight feather to confirm the age if the spur is intermediate. The bursa is located dorsally in the vent. Age determination in prairie grouse is covered in *Grouse of Plains and Mountains: The South Dakota Story* (see pg. 30). Use of the bursa for age determination is a difficult method even for most biologists unless you have someone to show you how. Pictures of adult and juvenile spurs on page 24 of the pheasant book (see above) are helpful for aging pheasants correctly.

Although I may remove the entrails during the day if it is hot, on most days I usually wait until I get back to where I am lodging. If I'm going to pick them it is easiest in the field right after shooting a bird but it is hard to stop the chase long enough for such activities. Pheasants and grouse have to be plucked carefully since the skin is notably thin and tears away easily. Another effective method for plucking birds is to plunge the birds in a bucket of nearly boiling water. That definitely makes the feathers easier to remove. That is the method I used on chickens and turkeys since early days on a farm.

If you pick, skin, or otherwise clean birds in the field I recommend you get away from the parking area or roadside so as not to leave an unsightly mess. Cleaning birds near the road also may give away your hunting spot. If you are on private land don't leave a mess of feathers and entrails around the farm buildings or home. You will still need to complete cleanup and packaging of the birds after returning to your place of lodging. When I lived in Brookings, I kept a heater in the garage just for staying warm while processing birds on cold days. A heater really helps reduce the misery when late fall and winter cold hit. A basement or washroom sink can be nice for final wash up of the processed birds if it is too cold to use an outside hose.

As a nonresident of South Dakota in recent years, I often freeze each pheasant or grouse in a gallon plastic bag until I travel home. If it is cool enough you could just gut the birds and let them age during your trip home. Depending on temperatures, I sometimes do this with birds taken during the last few days of my trip. On the trip home, I usually keep the frozen birds in the cooler and then wrap them in plastic wrap and freezer paper before putting them in the home freezer. During the hunt, some of the small-town motels that cater to hunters will have a freezer for keeping birds.

In my case, except for the plucked birds, processed birds do not usually look very professionally done. Skinned birds, by far the easiest method, never seem to look that nicely processed. Unlike chickens in the grocery store, wild harvested birds have blood and usually a few loose feather on the carcass after skinning, washing, and wrapping. I give skinned birds the extra cleaning just before I cook them. Plucked birds look much more appetizing. No harm done either way.

My father-in-law Ruel Allen and Pepsi on a Game Production Area near Brookings in the fall of 1980. We normally processed pheasants in our backyard, or, if especially cold, in the garage.

Ch. 74. These birds didn't come out of a grocery store

It seems like every year the President of the United States is given a turkey that he promptly pardons. I would like to see the President deny such a pardon for once and then to have the bird butchered and served up for Thanksgiving. I've denied plenty of pardons for poultry when I was a kid on the farm. I often got the job of killing and processing such birds. One thing nice about teaching at SDSU, most of the students were connected to the land and knew how to survive without a grocery store nearby.

Processing wild pheasants or grouse brings up a memorable occurrence. Mark and Joy were two of our good friends in Brookings. I sometimes took them a dressed pheasant for eating. For some reason, I was concerned at the time that their two daughters, Thalia-Rae and Allyssa-Rae, knew nothing about the wild game they were eating. Sort of like people eating professionally processed meat from the store. I thought it would be good for them if I brought a whole pheasant over to their garage and processed it with the girls watching. I could show them the various organs such as the gizzard, lungs, spleen, and heart, a bit like our bird dissection laboratory in ornithology except the girls did not do the actual dissecting.

I carried through with the idea and they watched attentively as I opened up a recently shot pheasant and showed them the various organs and even some of the major muscles. Before gutting the birds I showed them the external features, the feather tracks, the types of feathers, the spurs, and other aspects. Maybe I should have stopped right there! They seemed quite interested in everything I showed them and they probably were. However, they were also completely grossed out by the "blood and guts" of processing a real animal for eating. I still think it was a good lesson but it did cause them to stop eating pheasants for quite a long time. They clearly remember this demonstration and remind me when I see them on occasion.

Ch. 75. Don't overcook game birds

Over the years my family has eaten plenty of wild game including pheasants, prairie grouse species, gray partridge, mourning doves, ducks (many species), geese, deer, fish, and even snapping turtles. I did all the cooking and processing and hoped that the family would enjoy the wild game. Complaints that mourning dove breasts looked too much the size of our parakeet were common as were complaints that snapping turtles kept moving their legs hours after I had killed them by removing the head. Everyone liked pheasants and corn-fed white-tailed deer and, most liked prairie grouse. The decision on ducks was strongly split with Marcia, Margo (my oldest daughter), and three out of four Brittanys disliking the taste of any kind of duck and myself, Kim, and Ryan enjoying duck. None of the meat was wasted.

I even cleaned, cooked, and ate a crow that I shot near Lake Sinai, west of Brookings—it tasted pretty good. The idea to try crow came from an older professor, George Hudson, at Washington State University, when I was helping him teach the ornithology laboratory as a graduate student. He had told me of how young raven was excellent eating. Well, crow is a close cousin to ravens and can be legally shot in season so why not try one. No, I did not feed it to my family! As a youth I was acquainted with a teenage girl (and she was pretty) who was handy with a rifle and shotgun that told me robins feeding on their family strawberry patch were excellent eating. Maybe that was because they were illegal to kill. Another friend told me his father shot a great blue heron by accident and that it tasted awful even with the best roasting recipe.

In cooking upland birds or any bird my major suggestion is to be careful not to overcook so that the meat becomes dry. The cooking time in a frying pan, broiler, or barbeque between the meat being cooked enough to be safe and ruining the flavor by overcooking can be a matter of a minute. Some of my favorite recipes for pheasant and grouse involve simple preparations where I fry thinly pounded breast and thigh steaks that have been flattened and flavored with favorite spices. Some of these steaks take only a couple of minutes to cook using a frying pan and olive oil. I may also fry the legs (the thighs are favorite fare for me) instead of deboning and pounding out thigh steaks. Nothing is wasted. Some favorite seasonings I use include garlic salt, pepper, basil, and a touch of oregano but there are many possibilities. I mix the herbs and other flavorings with flour and dip or shake the steaks and other parts in the flour before frying. Done this way, the heart, liver, and gizzard are absolutely delicious right out of the frying pan. However, if you have an adult bird you might want to toss the liver since it could have elevated levels of pesticides.

Another favorite recipe with pheasant breasts is to take both breasts and flatten them with a meat pounder. Then place Swiss cheese (or other favorite cheese), sliced mushrooms, and sliced ham on the flattened steaks and roll them up as with chicken cordon bleu. Wooden toothpicks hold them in place. You can then fry or broil the pheasant cordon bleu and it makes an impressive meal. Plucked pheasant or prairie grouse cooked in a smoker is excellent. I use fruitwood from pruning fruit trees in my yard. Plucked pheasants and grouse are also excellent smoked in a more traditional manner after soaking in a brine solution.

I often cook older pheasants in a slow cooker with chicken bouillon and use the meat to make pheasant tacos, pheasant burritos, or pheasant enchiladas. One of my friends makes an excellent game bird jambalaya in a Dutch oven. There are lots of recipes for pheasants and grouse on the Internet and most chicken recipes work great with these birds.

Be careful about shot, especially if you use steel shot for everything like I do. You might even want to use some kind of metal finder to find those hidden steel pellets. The saying at wild bird dinners in our home was that you got the dishes if you found the first pellet. However, that really just remained a saying with no enforcement since I made a pretty big kitchen mess while cooking game and automatically earned clean up duties.

Ch. 76. As a nonresident—tripping to paradise and back

Sometime in late October of every year since I left South Dakota in August of 2002, I head east across Wyoming on my way to South Dakota. For the first nine years after I retired, I needed to visit South Dakota as part of my work on a series of three wildlife books and a technical report (*Mallard use of elevated nesting structures*) for the South Dakota Department of Game, Fish and Parks. Meeting with coauthors; taking photographs; and gathering data and photos on wild turkeys, pheasants, and grouse were all things I needed to get done. Each year I would stay almost three weeks and you can bet that bird hunting was a priority. Truth is, I would have made the trips to South Dakota anyway even without the work commitment. For me, there is still a deep connection to South Dakota and long-time friends are never really replaced.

If I leave my home in Springville at midday in late October I often stay at a private campground along the way that charges about $15—I can't see paying for a motel when I will be leaving seven or eight hours later. I have slept in my sleeping bag in a tent, under a pick-up topper, and in the tipped-back front seat of a jeep. It is usually pretty warm in late October.

On the way home I often try to hunt grouse early in the morning before departing western South Dakota, leaving time to reach Casper Wyoming late that evening. The temperatures are usually markedly colder and snow is not uncommon by time I make the return trip in the second week of November. If it is too cold I might be forced to get a motel. If it is only moderately cold I often stay in the tipped-back passenger seat in my vehicle for a small fee in a private campground. I have tried a Wal-Mart parking lot a couple of times but my friends tell me that may not be safe. I usually climb into my sleeping bag by 9:30 p.m., remaining fully clothed and with heavy socks on. The first time I tried sleeping in the tipped-back front seat on the way home I awoke around midnight with icy toes and tried to warm up by running the engine and heater for a short time. Then I had a better idea! I got my Brittany out of her kennel and put her on the floor in front of the passenger side front seat. She loved the attention. I then got back in my sleeping bag with a warm dog below my feet. Feet and toes stay toasty this way. The "warm dog" technique works perfectly for you and the dog.

If you are traveling a long distance as I do, it pays to find points of interest along the way to help stay alert, to make the trip more interesting, and to avoid potential blood flow problems from sitting too long. On a recent late October drive to South Dakota I stopped early in the morning to talk to a fly fisherman camped on the Platte River in Wyoming below Alcova Dam. His first words were: "Get your fly rod out right now!" He said he had caught and released over 60 nice rainbow trout using small nymphs the previous day. I didn't have my fly rod in the car but I watched him fish for a half hour and he was telling the truth. A one-day Wyoming fishing license and a few hours of fly fishing on the Platte make for a great travel break on my trips to South Dakota. Another good spot to stay and fish a few hours is Spearfish Creek in South Dakota. And believe me, it can be great fishing with a dry fly or nymph right in town, especially in the city park below the power plant where you can also camp. The stream has good-sized brown trout and lesser numbers of rainbow trout; the abundant brown trout are all hatched in the river. I still find the density of good sized brown trout in Spearfish Creek difficult to envision. They are unusually abundant!

Ch. 77. Neophyte hunters—a bit scary

Even with experienced hunters, carrying loaded firearms can always be dangerous. If I take a person I have not hunted with I watch them closely to see if they know how to safely use a shotgun. It is especially important to make sure accompanying hunters are careful about where the shotgun is pointed. I remain reluctant to hunt with a neophyte hunter and shooter. It can be dangerous and should be looked at as a training session and not a regular hunt. In one case I took my sisters 17-year old son on a hunt while he was staying at our home for the school year. I made sure he took hunter safety. He had also told me he was experienced with use of shotguns and hunting. He was not! An accidental blast from his shotgun a few feet behind me as we were leaving camp left both of us shaking and gave me reason to watch my nephew more closely and work with this young man on safety as the hunting season progressed. Glad I had stressed being careful that the barrel was not pointed at another hunter before we left camp. In a lifetime of hunting I have had two shotguns go off unintentionally, one as a teenager with a difficult to pull hammer on a 12-gauge single shot (hammer slipped), and the other on a "hang fire" while goose hunting with two friends—sure glad I had remembered the rule of always pointing the barrel away from people and hunting dogs.

One instant sign that you could be in danger and that the person is not an experienced hunter is when they start touching off extra-long shots at birds that are far out of range. One day we had three hunters from California that the landowner wanted Chad Lehman (my former Ph.D. student) and me to take hunting on his land. One of them was clearly a first-time hunter as we could tell when he fired at a hen pheasant (illegal) that passed over him in clear view and then followed that by emptying his shotgun (normal factory loads) at a distant rooster with three shots fired at from 75 to 200 yards. This is not an exaggeration! I'm sure there was no danger to the distant rooster even on the

75-yard shot but the incident was a red flag. Chad and I soon managed to end the hunt and excuse ourselves.

Those of you who have ever acted as a guide on commercial hunting areas have plenty of stories related to inexperienced bird hunters. You too may have feared for your own safety and for that of your hunting dog.

Ch. 78. Chinook salmon and prairie grouse

It was sometime in the 1990s during summer and I was with Gary Marrone from Pierre, trolling for chinook salmon with downriggers in Lake Oahe. My 8 weight fly rod was set in a rod holder and was strongly bent by the pull of the water against the belly of my sinking fly line. In fact, the entire fly line and part of the backing were under water, bowed by the force of the water. About 70 feet below a rubber band held the whole stressed fly line in place with the trailing flasher and an artificial squid. What kind of idiotic way was this to use a fly fishing setup? And to think some fly fishing purists will use only a dry fly. I had become most wayward in terms of true fly fishing but then I just had to find out what a salmon felt like on a nine-foot fly rod.

About that time my fly line kicked loose from the downrigger connection (rubber band) and I felt the strength of a powerful chinook salmon running with the soft plastic squid. It was a crazy fight with the 9 foot rod bent close to the maximum and the single action fly reel spinning out of control at times, the crank handle threatening to break a finger or my thumb. On spirited runs, I tried to slow the salmon by putting my thumb on the spool of backing or fly line in the reel and soon felt a white hot burning sensation on my flesh. The drag was totally insufficient for the power of the fish. I eventually landed a 10-pound salmon and a couple more of similar size on that crazy fly rod-downrigger setup. It was a thrill and I have since followed it up with five fly fishing trips to Alaska to catch silver salmon (cohos), sockeye salmon (reds), and pink salmon using a more traditional fly fishing approach with colorful nymphs and streamers. They will all hit wet flies if you use the right colors. Don't be fooled by those who tell you it is necessary to snag sockeyes to get them. Those folks just don't know how to fish sockeyes in the most sporting way and plenty of them stick with less sporting and often illegal snagging techniques. As for silvers, they will come several feet out of the way to put a vicious hit on a nymph or streamer. Pinks are the easiest of all to catch when the runs are in progress. Most of the time purple marabou (or chartreuse) trailed by pink marabou for a tail are my deadliest flies for salmon and they are easy to tie. I'll bet they would work in Lake Oahe if you got them close to those chinook salmon.

Pierre is a dream place to live in if you are a hunter or angler and I love the times I have spent there. The fishing is always good and access to pheasant and grouse hunting is unbeatable. The main-stem reservoirs in South Dakota provide a tremendous fishery that includes walleye, northern pike, white bass, smallmouth bass, and chinook salmon. The idea of a chinook salmon fishery in a prairie state may seem a little strange. However, they are present in the Oahe Reservoir in good numbers during most years. The chinook salmon population in Oahe is maintained by using a salmon spawning station where the salmon run up a raceway ladder and are spawned inside the hatchery building. Most of the mature chinook salmon are in the seven to 12-pound range but a few have surpassed 20 lbs. Not so big compared to the Great Lakes or the Alaskan chinook salmon populations but pretty nice for a prairie reservoir.

Gary Marrone took me on several fishing trips on the Oahe Reservoir for chinook salmon and, in the tailwaters for walleye and giant white bass. Gary had encouraged me to use the unorthodox fly rod approach for salmon on Lake Oahe after a May trip on the tail waters where I was catching large white bass (14-15 inches) on a six-weight fly rod and chartreuse and white streamer (Clauser's minnow). On one of our fishing trips on Lake Oahe we ended up catching our limit of 5 chinook salmon apiece. Gary loaded my cooler with all 10 salmon to take home to Brookings. He also told George Vandel, the Director of the Wildlife Division (now retired), about our great day of salmon fishing and that I was headed back to Brookings with those fish. I had known George since he was a graduate student at South Dakota State and I can safely say he always had a very good sense of humor. George could not resist calling one of my friends and colleagues at South Dakota State University, Ken Higgins, and telling him I was headed back to Brookings with a bumper crop of fresh salmon for everyone. The next day, folks in my Department were waiting for their salmon fillets.

I often took my fly rod on grouse hunts and combined fishing and hunting activities. I have hit some stock ponds loaded with largemouth bass that would readily take a deer hair popper, or a black wooly bugger. On one September hunt near Murdo, I had my limit of sharptails by 10:00 a.m. and spent the rest of the day catching beautiful largemouth bass in a private stock pond using my fly rod. Other fish often found in stock ponds include bluegills, rainbow trout, crappie, yellow perch, and even northern pike. If you are hunting near Gettysburg in late September or early October, Whitlock Bay can be loaded with chinook salmon moving towards the salmon spawning station. The salmon are usually close to shore at this time and shore fisherman catch them on spinners, crank baits, and even large colorful flies. Many of the northeastern lakes are loaded with walleye, northern pike, small mouth bass, white bass and other species that can provide fast action in the fall. Most of the larger water bodies have public access. Stock ponds with decent populations of game fish can be found on public lands such as the Fort Pierre National Grassland or on private ranches. Most ranchers are good about allowing you to fish. If you are planning a hunting trip in September and even through October, you might want to bring along some fishing gear.

Part VII. Threats to the South Dakota paradise

Ch. 79. Wetlands, wildlife, and sinking duck boats

From the first year we moved to eastern South Dakota in 1972 I found beauty in the rolling glacial hills, agricultural landscape, and especially, the interspersed wetlands. These wetlands varied from small areas that held water only during a month or so in the spring to larger marshes that held water in most years. The emergent vegetation in these wetlands was likewise diverse and related to the water regime (permanence of standing water) as well as other factors. During spring and summer, wetlands often provided a cacophony of bird sounds because of the abundance and variety of bird life dependent on these areas for food and cover.

Since that time in the early 1970s I have accumulated uncounted memories of ring-necked pheasants flushing from dense wetland cover, especially when snow covers the landscape. Some of those would flush so close I could have practically caught them with a long-handled fishing net. I know how important wetland cover is for pheasants throughout the year, especially dense cattails, phragmites, and willow clumps that can kill the chilling winds during cold and snowy days.

Surprisingly, some landowners and many of the state's citizens do not realize how important dense wetland cover is to pheasants and other wildlife throughout the year. One landowner friend told me he was considering draining an approximately four-acre wetland that I often hunted in the winter. The wintering pheasants concentrated in the dense cattails that covered over half of the wetland basin. When I commented that he would lose this valuable wintering habitat for pheasants, his reply was that the pheasants could winter in his adjacent alfalfa. Obviously, there is no break at all from the chilling winter winds in the regrowth of a second- or third-cut alfalfa field. Fortunately, the wetland was still there last time I checked.

In the appropriate seasons, wetland habitat supports a host of other species including migrating and reproducing waterfowl, wintering white-tailed deer, pied-billed grebes, marsh wrens, sora rails, yellow-headed blackbirds, mink, muskrats, and lots of other wildlife. Wetlands along with native prairie get my vote for eastern South Dakota's most valuable wildlife oases.

I have spent much time in these valuable wetlands, especially during pheasant and waterfowl seasons and have already shared many memories of bird hunting in wetlands in earlier chapters. Other wetland memories also run deep. Sinking a couple of duck boats gave me some new looks at larger wetlands from the water surface level. One sinking was during an early Canada goose hunt in the 1990s with Carter Johnson and Gary Peterson in a marsh (Fox Slough) near Astoria. Our duck boat was overloaded with three hunters, floating goose decoys, geese, ammunition boxes, and other gear as we slowly motored back to the launch point following our goose hunt. Without our noticing, the bow of the boat began to sink due to the overload and headed to the bottom of the shallow marsh. I can remember wading up to the nearby shore with my water-filled neoprene boots increasingly ballooning out like the Michelin man (in the commercial) as I tried to exit the water. I felt like I weighed over 400 pounds. Carter and Gary were laughing hysterically. If you wonder what it looked like just try wading too deep in neoprene waders (no belt around the waist) and then walking back out on the shore (see sketch on following page). We did rescue the shotguns before the boat went down and had no problem saving the boat and other articles.

It was about sunrise on an early November day in the 1980s, again on Fox Slough near Astoria. Vic Myers and I were tossing out our decoys in a gorgeous open area near heavy cattail cover where we had flushed several hundred ducks, mostly mallards. I can still feel the chills when my friend Vic Myers reached out from my flat-bottomed, 14-foot duck boat to straighten up a

Sophia Shaw

tipped mallard decoy; the boat flipped in a flash and dumped hunters, shotguns, and everything in the boat in over four feet of water. Decoys look different bobbing in your face from a water level view! Standing in water over the top of your chest waders and looking up at a large flock of mallards circling the decoys was a most unique experience. The setup probably looked pretty good to the mallards while we were still in the water. A sort of sink-box decoy setup! I recall getting the boat upright, pushing Vic back into the boat, using my feet to lift up shotguns from the bottom sediments and rebagging already deployed decoys. Our metal ammunition boxes floated because they were still latched but the lunches got soaked. I couldn't get back in the boat so I just pulled the boat and waded to shore about 80 yards away.

On the shore we wrung out clothes the best we could, poured the water out of our waders, and reorganized. Insanely, since the temperatures were relatively warm for early November (about 55 degrees Fahrenheit), we actually went back, set out a few decoys, and tried to hunt in our soaked condition. I think the dunking must have addled our minds a bit. We lasted less than half an hour before shivering signaled we had best pick up and paddle back to the launch area. This early November sinking could have been dangerous had the water been deeper and the day colder.

Sophia Shaw

Such memories just further my attachment to these great wildlife areas. Oh yes, in both sinkings, the ring-necked pheasants, as always, were crowing in the peripheral shoreline vegetation of the wetland.

Spending a few hours quietly watching the behaviors of the many animal species using these marshes can be a rewarding and educational experience. In spring, wetlands were always a prime spot for taking my ornithology classes since these areas supported so much bird life. One fun field experience was to tie a pair of black socks with red patches onto the top of a cattail spike. The dummy attracted nearby male red-winged blackbirds that attacked and sometimes knocked the red-patched dummy off of the cattail spike in defense of their territory. I still wish I had tried dressing up in a black cape with red patches on the shoulders for one of these ornithology trips. I suspect the male red-winged blackbirds would have attacked the "red-shouldered giant" regardless of size. I loved teaching ornithology and field trips were the most fun of all.

Those who have hunted pheasants, white-tailed deer, and waterfowl often have a particular appreciation for the value of wetlands. For me, I am incurably attracted to these beautiful glacial wetlands, my mind filled with memories of so many experiences with wildlife and friends over the past 40 years.

In some ways, glacial wetlands in eastern South Dakota have a similar natural beauty to the mountains of Colorado, trout rivers of Montana, or even the coastline of Oregon. I continue to see glacial wetlands as an integral part of the very beauty and fabric of eastern South Dakota; they give the landscape character and make the place more enjoyable to live. In the words of one of North America's most esteemed naturalists Paul L. Errington: "Yet for me as an individual, no other natural feature has ever had the enduring attraction of an undespoiled chain of marshes in an undespoiled setting of glacial hills" (Paul L. Errington. 1957. *Of Men and Marshes*). Paul Errington grew up just northwest of Brookings near Oakwood Lakes. I was involved in establishing the Paul L. Errington Memorial Marsh and setting up a plaque there in the 1970s with fellow faculty Alan Wentz and Chuck Scalet. We mounted the plaque in a concoction of cement with glacial stones to make it look attractive. When I last checked, the bronze memorial plaque and the glacial-stone masonry were still there and in good shape. Fittingly, 292 acres on the shores of Johnson Lake (most westerly of Oakwood Lakes complex) were recently (2012) donated by the Errington family as a Waterfowl Production Area and prairie preserve.

I'm grateful for the private wetlands that are protected from drainage or filling through the U.S. Fish and Wildlife Service Wetland Easements Program and other programs such as the U.S. Department of Agriculture's Wetland Reserve Program. I also am appreciative of wetlands and surrounding uplands purchased as Game Production Areas (state) and Waterfowl Production Areas (federal) with funding largely from hunters.

Finding Paradise in South Dakota

Hunters and others who enjoy eastern South Dakota's natural beauty should be especially appreciative of landowners that have resisted draining wetlands and have made efforts to protect them.

Unfortunately, hunters driving to their favorite pheasant hunting spots in eastern South Dakota will very likely see coils of black drainage tile, much of it poised for use in draining remaining unprotected wetlands. They may also see the remnants of wetland areas and moist drainages that they may have hunted or noticed in previous years but that are now gone. Several new drainage tile industries have sprung up in recent years in South Dakota's cities and towns to support this increasing effort to drain wetlands. Pheasant populations and other wildlife have suffered greatly from these wetland losses as well as other recent losses of Conservation Reserve and other grasslands in eastern South Dakota. Beautifully illustrated advertisements coupling use of drainage tile and resulting "wildlife-friendly" landscapes are a great falsehood. These advertisements represent highly deceptive advertising in regard to their influence on beautiful landscapes and wildlife in South Dakota. Without doubt, wetland drainage is destructive for ring-necked pheasants, waterfowl, and most other wildlife. Tile operations and pheasants do not go together!

Sadly, South Dakota becomes less beautiful, less diverse, and more flood prone with each wetland loss. As drainage tile is installed in unprotected wetlands (and many fields), the water that would have remained in these small wetlands is rapidly transported down the watershed where it causes unwanted downstream flooding of our river systems, lakes, and remaining wetlands. People downstream or lower in the watershed often end up suffering economically because of drainage in other parts of the watershed. Every part of the land seems linked. One only need note the record-breaking floods that are ever more common in the Midwest to realize it would be much wiser to keep water in the thousands of glacially formed wetlands that originally existed. Pheasants and most other wildlife species would strongly agree if they had a voice in the matter!

Ch. 80. More row crops and less cover mean fewer pheasants

Pheasants are well adapted to agriculture as long as adequate amounts of undisturbed grass-forb cover and other nonuse areas remain available. In fact, pheasants need agriculture and the associated waste grain it provides. Pheasants are certainly much more adapted to loss of grassland cover than prairie grouse since prairie grouse pretty much disappear when less than 50% of the landscape is covered with grassland in reasonably good condition. Pheasants will not likely be completely eliminated from an area by intensive row crop farming but the numbers of pheasants in areas of intensive agriculture will be much lower than in landscapes that still have plenty of cowboy-boot high or higher grassland or other nonuse cover available. A farmland with 30% of the landscape in decent pheasant nesting and brood rearing cover (concealing grasses and forbs) is far more productive for pheasants than one with only 10%. In fact, pheasant roadside surveys in South Dakota indicate that pheasant densities are highest in areas of South Dakota that have around 50-60% grassland on the landscape and 40% cropland (see *Ring-necked Pheasants: Thriving in South Dakota*, pg. 106).

Even though waste grain is important as food for upland game birds, don't make the mistake of thinking that row crops such as corn, sorghum, or sunflowers can serve as nesting cover for pheasants, sharp-tailed grouse, or greater prairie-chickens. Such areas are nesting deserts and basically add nothing to the annual hatch of these upland game birds. They are also biological deserts for other prairie nesting birds like mallards and various grassland songbirds. Most row crops are also poor habitat for pheasant or prairie grouse broods in the critical first four to five weeks of life because of their need for insects as food as well as secure escape cover. This early chick age is when the chicks are most vulnerable to mortality. If an area looks like it is almost entirely made up of row crops, as in some areas of eastern South Dakota, don't expect there to be many pheasants.

Winter wheat, in contrast, can support moderate densities of nesting pheasants although it is not as good as grass-forb nesting cover. Winter wheat can also be quite good cover for broods and full-sized pheasants if tall stubble (15 inches or more) is retained along with green manure plantings or volunteer weed growth. If left standing, tall w heat stubble provides good habitat in the fall and in mild winters and it improves soil moisture by collecting drifting snow (see Ch. 14. *Ring-necked Pheasants: Thriving in South Dakota*). Tall stubble also keeps drifting snow out of downwind winter cover for pheasants and other wildlife.

In the early 1900s when pheasants were first introduced the mixture of cropland with grassland and wetland habitat was optimal for these birds. Since the first hunting season in 1920, pheasants have especially thrived during periods when idle farmland, weedy cover, and grassland were abundant. Abundance of idle farmland and grassland nesting cover in periods such as the 1930s (Great Depression), World War II, The Soil Bank Years (mid 1950s to mid 1960s), and the recent Conservation Reserve Program have been associated with peaks of pheasant abundance (see *Ring Necked Pheasants: Thriving in South Dakota*. Chapter 1).

As the percentage of the landscape in intensive use for row crops increases, nesting success and numbers of pheasants will decline—you can bank on it. Just look at pheasant numbers in heavily farmed portions of Illinois, Iowa, and Indiana if you need proof. These states clearly show that more corn, soybeans, and other row crops and fewer wetlands and grasslands mean fewer pheasants. Larger crop field sizes and less diverse crops also usually mean fewer pheasants. For that reason, the recent replacement of Conservation Reserve Program grasslands (CRP) and other areas of good pheasant cover in eastern South Dakota with corn, soybeans, or other row crops has caused a serious decline in the pheasant population. Sharp-tailed grouse and greater prairie-chickens populations are also being negatively affected by losses of CRP and other grassland cover. Both of these grouse species were beginning to expand their distribution in northeastern South Dakota during the peak years of the CRP in the early 2000s. The influence of increased corn and soybean production in causing wetland drainage and loss of hundreds of thousands of acres of grassland cover is well documented in post CRP years. (see Wright, C. K. and M. C. Wimberly. *2013. Recent land use change in the Western Corn Belt threatens grasslands and wetlands.* search Internet under title; Reitsma, et al. 2014. Estimated South Dakota land use change from 2006-2012. IGrow: SDSU Extension Service. SDSU Department of Plant Science, Brookings.) The effect of these grassland and wetland losses on wildlife is devastating and widespread in South Dakota and the midwest. Pheasant and prairie grouse populations in South Dakota are showing the effects of these habitat losses.

Pheasant hunters should look for landscapes that still have abundant grass and forb cover for nesting and brood rearing habitat. In your pheasant abundance equation remember that intermixed fields of winter wheat and tall wheat stubble can also produce significant numbers of pheasants. Although pheasants will sometimes move a few miles to find winter cover, they tend to remain within a mile or less of where they hatch during most of the fall. So look for agricultural landscapes where crops are intermixed with plentiful grasslands, wetlands, and other cover for the best pheasant areas. Where cropland exists intermixed with over 50% grassland on the landscape, there is a good chance that the area supports prairie grouse in addition to ring-necked pheasants. These areas with mixed species of upland game birds are among my favorites when hunting in South Dakota.

Ch. 81. Disappearing native grasslands, prairie grouse, and memories

It was late October in 2011 and I was headed for some favorite grouse hunting areas west of the Missouri River in northern South Dakota. One of my favorite ranch areas was a walk-in area of nearly three square miles but I noted that it was no longer shown on the hunting atlas. Still, I was looking forward to seeing that ranch and perhaps checking with the rancher to see if he would allow me to hunt sharptails. Sharp-tailed grouse were abundant on that ranch in past years and the hunting and gun dog work phenomenal. The last time I had hunted there the rancher had told me he was considering selling the large ranch and asked if I was interested. Unfortunately, such a purchase could only be a dream for me.

Arriving at this favorite grouse hunting area I could see nothing but mature sunflowers covering over 2,000 acres of former sharp-tailed grouse habitat on both sides of the highway. All that grassland gone, the grouse dancing grounds (leks) gone, the native plants gone, the other prairie wildlife gone or shuffled to the ever dwindling adjacent grasslands. I was stunned but I should not have been because this same type of conversion is happening in many of South Dakota's better sharp-tailed grouse and greater prairie-chicken habitats.

In the last 40 years and especially in the last 15 years I have watched much classic ranchland and prairie grouse country fall to the plow or to chemical conversion to cropland. According to research at South Dakota State University (SDSU), over 1,837,000 acres of grassland, including Conservation Reserve Program plantings, pastures, native grasslands, and miscellaneous grasslands, were converted to other uses in South Dakota from 2006 to 2011. Of those acres, 1,439,500 were converted to cropland (see Reitsma, et al., 2014. Estimated South Dakota land use change from 2006-2012. IGrow: SDSU Extension Service. SDSU Department of Plant Science, Brookings).

Unfortunately, row crops like corn, soybeans, and sunflowers receive basically no use by nesting pheasants, prairie grouse, ducks, or other birds. Winter wheat, an exception, can provide nesting cover for pheasants, ducks, and some other bird species (see *Ring-necked Pheasants: Thriving in South Dakota*, pgs. 216-218).

As noted earlier, the plants found in native prairies cannot be restored in full after these areas are turned into cropland although they can be partially restored by planting available native seeds. Restoration efforts are still worthwhile. Time will surely show that recently converted native prairies should not have been destroyed in the first place. Far too much marginal and thin soil has been left open to wind and water erosion. Even if farmed with minimum tillage and no-till farming methods, I question the sanity of native prairie destruction on most of these recently converted lands. By putting crops on marginal lands, we are mining those marginal surface soils and leaving nothing for the future. They need protective grass!

On some of the native grassland areas on river-break topography, the thin top soils have been plowed on slopes so steep that one can readily envision the impending erosion with coming rain storms. In many cases, large corporations are purchasing these fragile grasslands from struggling or retiring ranchers and replacing the grassland with tillage and cropland. Unfortunately, over the years loopholes in federal crop disaster programs have made such destructive practices economically advantageous in the short term to large corporations or others who care little about the future of South Dakota's soil and grassland resources in these marginal farming areas. However, progress is being made in modifying the negative aspects of these federal crop disaster programs. These modifications (as of 2014) will hopefully reverse the trend to convert marginal soils, native grasslands, and seeded grasslands to cropland.

Conversion of native grassland to cropland using chemicals or plowing is generally a fairly rapid process. Great effort and expense is needed for even partial restoration of these native prairies. Without protective grass cover, the thin, marginal soils on many of these tilled areas can so easily end up blowing and washing away, deposited in road ditches, ravines, rivers, and canyons where they were not meant to be.

I would like to see the playing field leveled to give ranchers a better chance at keeping the states precious soils protected by grasslands. Too many federal programs have unintentionally spurred the conversion of native grasslands and other grasslands to cropland. My dream for South Dakota would be for ranching lands to begin expanding in areas of central and western South Dakota where too much prairie has already been destroyed. In the great Dust Bowl this type of reclamation was used to save soils and return prosperity to the land. The many ranchers that are dedicated to keeping their land primarily in native grassland are the greatest hope for prairie grouse, other prairie wildlife, for the precious soil, and for the diverse plants that make up the prairie. Many tribal lands also provide hope for retaining native prairies. Some cropland mixed in with extensive prairie, especially in the better soil areas, is manageable in terms of keeping our prairie wildlife and soils but extensive tillage of thin, marginal soils is a great danger. It seems we have forgotten old lessons that the grass, wind, water, and soil have taught us. We are painfully slow to learn lessons from the land, especially from our native prairies, and continually repeat the mistakes of the past.

With land prices skyrocketing, the trend in conversion of our protective grassland cover is not unexpected. There have obviously been few or no effective penalties or rewards in federal farm programs for greatly slowing or stopping destruction of planted or native grassland. In marginal soil areas, the penalty will come with drifting soil across fence lines, dark skies filled with blowing top soil, silted lakes and streams, and future dust bowls.

Ch. 82. Still a paradise for bird hunting

Hunters planning to visit South Dakota will find some recent trends discouraging in terms of loss of pheasant and grouse habitat. However, if you love hunting upland game birds there is still plenty of reason to plan a trip to South Dakota. In general I would tend to avoid the more heavily farmed counties on the eastern edge of the state for pheasant hunting unless farming practices or land retirement systems reverse the current trend of loss of grasslands and wetlands. However, hunters can usually find hot spots even in the poorer pheasant counties (based on annual brood surveys) plus these counties often have minimal competition from other hunters even on public areas.

If you are a nonresident, even the poorer pheasant counties in eastern South Dakota usually have more pheasants than the better areas in your home state. That certainly holds true for Utah where I now live. For these reasons and because of friends living there, I still spend part of my hunting trip to South Dakota hunting pheasants in some of the counties with the greatest recent loss of wildlife habitat and the poorest pheasant populations.

In recent years I spend more time closer to the Missouri River or even in western South Dakota hunting a combination of pheasants and prairie grouse. This portion of the state has a higher proportion of grassland remaining with many counties having over 40% of the landscape still in grass cover. At 60% grassland (most of the remainder in cropland) the landscape can support great pheasant hunting and still have healthy numbers of greater prairie-chickens (central and south-central regions) and sharp-tailed grouse. My rule of thumb is that prairie grouse tend to disappear from landscapes with less than 50% grassland and are basically absent (rare) from areas with less than 40% grassland as in much of southeastern South Dakota. These estimates have been confirmed by recent research at SDSU on prairie grouse occurrence in relation to grassland cover on the landscape (Personal communication, Kent Jensen; Orth, Mandy R. 2012. M.S. Thesis, South Dakota State University). Prairie grouse and their range in the state will decline as grasslands on remaining marginal lands, especially native grasslands, are unwisely tilled or chemically treated and replaced with cropland.

Counties that have retained a more favorable ratio of grassland to cropland remain strongholds for pheasants. Isolated areas along or west of the Missouri River remain some of my favorites because of the mixture of pheasants and prairie grouse available.

Hunters interested in pursuing sharp-tailed grouse will find plenty of large walk-in areas in western South Dakota where they can escape the pheasant hunters and be alone and into good sharp-tailed grouse hunting. Some of these walk-in areas cover thousands of acres. Productive greater prairie-chicken hunting is more limited to the central portions of the state near the Missouri River in areas such as the Fort Pierre National Grassland (see *Grouse of Plains and Mountains: The South Dakota Story*). Most areas with greater prairie-chickens will also have sharp-tailed grouse. As a rule, if an area is good for prairie grouse but has very few pheasants (grassland landscapes), there will be few or no other upland bird hunters after the opening weekend of the grouse season.

Watching a hunting dog work across a native prairie for grouse is a remarkable and memorable experience. It makes me feel like I have come home to an old and trusted landscape, an old friend. In 2013, I stopped for my first South Dakota hunt of the year on mixed-grass prairie near Phillip. I'm an overly emotional person anyway (like at some movies) but as I walked across that prairie with my Brittany working ahead of me for grouse and pheasants I had to stop, gather my thoughts, and revel in the deep emotions I felt for that moment and the scene in front of me. Enjoy the native prairies now, for we are unwisely losing native grassland much too rapidly.

Time spent hunting upland birds in South Dakota is a priceless experience. The more you hunt the state (assuming you get out and walk), the more you will discover the remarkable opportunities for quality upland game bird hunting. And don't think it takes big bucks to hunt South Dakota. You can find plenty of public access areas with good hunting without paying commercial fees. In many areas, private landowners are good about allowing hunting, especially if you are not asking permission on the opening weekend and if you are not with a group of more than two or three. Permission to hunt on private land is granted more readily if you avoid the most popular pheasant counties. You can of course have some excellent hunts, food, and lodging on commercial pheasant hunting areas if you have the funds. Regardless of where you hunt, just make sure you avoid hunting in larger groups if you want to experience the quality type hunts I espouse in this book. For me, hunting alone or with one other person, both with a gun dog, is perfect.

If you are reading this book, you are probably mostly interested in finding places to hunt on available public lands, private lands leased by the state for hunting (such as walk-in areas), or by locating private landowners and asking permission to hunt. You are also likely intent on hunting alone or with one or two others, on walking plenty of cover, and on working your own hunting dog or dogs. If this type of hunt interests you then get out and enjoy South Dakota's appreciable upland bird hunting. If you don't live there then it is worth making the trip and staying for a week or more. Don't expect easy hunts but if you have a hunting dog that can find birds I can tell you they will be exciting hunts. The birds are wild, wild, wild, and the chase is exhilarating. You will make new friends with great people. South Dakota, I love it, you will love it, your gun dog will love it. It is paradise!

With a gun dog you can still find good pheasant hunting on South Dakota's public lands and walk-in areas.

Sharp-tailed grouse hunting in western South Dakota can make for a memorable hunting trip. (Courtesy of Doug Backlund).

Ch. 83 Epilogue

It is October 2014 and this book is ready for printing. Last month our Brittany, Brook, died of a sudden illness in her 11th year—she is greatly missed by Marcia and me. We buried her in a small grove of native big-tooth maple in our back yard, accompanied by colored stones and decorations made by our neighborhood children. Lots of great memories of points and retrieves but I most miss the hiking companion, the constant shadow following me around the yard and house, and the greeting we received at every opportunity. Brook had nicely pointed a covey of California quail near my favorite hiking trail just a week before she died.

I got my first Brittany in the spring 41 years ago after we moved to South Dakota. At 73 years old (Marcia is 4 years younger), I'm still thinking I have lots more hiking left and a few more years of bird hunting. Marcia figures I will live longer and be healthier if I have a gun dog companion to urge me to hike five or six days per week. Believe me, gun dogs will urge you to take them on a hike every day! Marcia started looking for Brittany pups within a few days after Brook died, found an impressive line (good hunters, friendly, and hopefully not too hyperactive), and got me to take a visit. We now have a new Brittany pup, Dakota. We somewhat knew the genetic lines because my daughter and son-in-law (Margo and Mike Shaw) had purchased their dog at the same place. I like several other gun dog breeds as well but I've had good luck with Brittanys so I'm staying the course. I'm hoping this pup will grow up to be a lot like Brook as a pet and gun dog. Brook was unusually calm.

For this fall I will borrow Margo and Mike's 5-year-old Brittany, Coco, for the South Dakota trip. To do so took getting permission from my 12-year-old granddaughter Eva. They live in Granite Bay, California and they don't hunt with Coco but she has good instincts so I'm hoping I can make it work. Coco does respond to the basic commands (heel, stay, come, etc.) and occasionally points song birds and tree squirrels in their yard. It will be a challenge but she will find birds I am sure. I'm hoping she will start pointing pheasants and grouse with a little on the job training. And I can't leave the new puppy home so that should also spice up the coming trip.

The pheasant brood survey reports for South Dakota indicate a strong year for reproduction in 2014 in portions of the state with decent habitat. I don't expect the hunting for pheasants and prairie grouse to be as good as during the peak years of the Conservation Reserve Program, but it will be good. Just hunting in South Dakota and seeing friends again will be good. It is always good enough for me.

My fifth Brittany, Dakota, at 9 weeks as of mid October 2014. She is already a good hiking companion but with much to learn.

Partial glossary of terms

Birdy: Term used in this book for any hunting dog that has picked up the scent of pheasants, grouse, or other upland game birds. Often evident from tail wagging or movements of the head as they detect and follow bird scent.

Bursa of Fabricius: A dorsal pocket just inside the vent (dorsally in the chamber called a cloaca) that is present in young birds but disappears or becomes shallow in adult birds.

Conservation Officer: Professional wildlife officers with multiple responsibilities in wildlife and fisheries law enforcement, wildlife surveys, land management, and public relations. Most South Dakota counties have at least one conservation officer.

Conservation Reserve Enhancement Program (CREP): This program involves U.S. Department of Agriculture funding and partial matching funds from the SDGFP. This program established up to 100,000 acres of undisturbed grassland for the benefit of soil, water, and wildlife and is open to public hunting on foot.

Conservation Reserve Program (CRP): A federal land retirement program that retired millions of acres of cropland into protective grass cover beginning in 1985. Acreages in CRP began a major decline about 2007.

East River: Land east of the Missouri River in South Dakota.

Emergent cover: Emergent vegetation that provides protective cover for pheasants, deer, and other wildlife in flooded, frozen, or periodically dry wetland basins. Also used to support the attached grass nests of birds such as yellow-headed blackbirds. Cattails are a type of dense emergent cover used heavily by pheasants and deer, especially in winter.

Emergent vegetation: Rooted aquatic plants, such as river bulrush or cattails, that grow through the water column and project above its surface in wetlands.

Forb: A herbaceous plant such as pasqueflower, Maxmillian sunflower, or, kochia (fireweed) that is not a grass or is not grasslike.

Game Production Area (GPA): Land purchased and managed as wildlife habitat by the South Dakota Department of Game, Fish and Parks with monies from state hunting licenses and a federal tax (shared with the states) on arms and ammunition. These areas are marked by signs and are open to public hunting.

Hemimarsh. A term sometimes used for a wetland that has about half open surface water and half emergent vegetation. Used very generally here for any wetland with an appreciable interspersion of open water and emergent vegetation.

Hot on scent or hot scent: Where the upland bird dog has clearly picked up the scent trail of a bird that is near. See definition of "birdy."

Meandered lakes: Meandered lakes were plotted as lakes when the federal government surveyed the land before statehood. Non-meandered lakes were not plotted as meandered by the federal government. South Dakota Department of Game, Fish and Parks argues that the public has the right to use meandered lakes and to hunt within the normal high water line of dry meandered lakes. They also argue the public has the right to hunt on flooded meandered lakes even if they have grown beyond their original size if they can be accessed from public property (roads, section lines) or from other public water such as other meandered lakes (as lakes grow together).

Mixed-grass prairie: A native prairie common to untilled lands over much of South Dakota other than the eastern and western edges. This grassland category includes the northern mixed-grass prairie and northern wheatgrass needlegrass plains (see J. R. Johnson and G. E. Larson. *Grassland plants of South Dakota and the Northern Great Plains*. Bulletin 566. South Dakota Agricultural Experiment Station, Brookings).

National grassland: Land owned by the federal government and managed on a multiple use basis by the U.S. Forest Service. These extensive landscapes are open to legal public hunting. The three major national grasslands in South Dakota are the Fort Pierre National Grassland, the Buffalo Gap National Grassland, and the Grand River National Grassland.

Population. All the individuals of one species within a specified area at a given time. For example, one could refer to the population of sharp-tailed grouse in the northern plains states or the population of walleye in Oahe Reservoir.

Prairie grouse: Species of grouse common to the plains. The term is used to refer to sharp-tailed grouse and greater prairie-chickens in South Dakota but technically could include the small population of greater sage-grouse found in western South Dakota.

Radio transmitter: A small device that can be attached to an organism such as a pheasant or deer that puts out a recognizable signal that can be picked up by researchers using a radio receiver. Often used to study movements and behavior. For example, radio transmitters are often attached to large gallinaceous species like pheasants using a poncho type mount that fits over the neck.

Residual vegetation: Above ground parts from plants such as grasses or forbs that are dead and are often from the previous year. For example, residual grass is important cover for ground nesting birds in the spring before new growth provides sufficient hiding cover.

Shelterbelts: Tree belts planted primarily for wind protection on farmlands. Shelterbelts may vary from single row belts to wide belts made of multiple rows of trees and shrubs.

South Dakota Department of Game, Fish and Parks: The state agency with broad responsibility for management of wildlife, fisheries, and parks. Headquarters are in Pierre. Not the same as the U.S. Fish and Wildlife Service.

South Dakota State University: Land grant university established in 1881 in Brookings South Dakota, about 50 miles north of Sioux Falls.

State School lands: South Dakota's school lands are "trust lands" granted to the state on its admission to the Union and total approximately 750,000 acres. These trust lands are leased and managed to produce income for the support of the state's schools, universities and other endowed institutions. School lands are open to public hunting and fishing without permission but it is still good policy to contact the leaseholder if nearby.

Restrictions include no hunting in standing crops or at distances of less than 660 feet from livestock and occupied buildings.

Succession in wetlands: Changes in wetland characteristics from year to year or more often over a period of several years or even over many decades. Successional stages in more permanent wetlands may include cycling from open water (flooded stages) with little or no emergent vegetation to nearly dry wetland basins with dense stands of emergent and drawdown vegetation. Succession greatly influences the wildlife (and fish) use of such wetlands. Some extensive wetlands covered with drawdown and emergent vegetation in the early 1980s are large fishing lakes today. Drainage of smaller wetlands has caused increased flooding of larger wetlands and has thus influenced the long-term successional patterns.

Tallgrass prairie: Native prairie originally found in the more moist, eastern edge of South Dakota. Characterized by native grasses such as big bluestem, Indian grass, and switch grass that can sometimes grow to the height of most hunters.

Upland game birds: Term used for quail, grouse, pheasants, partridge, and other gallinaceous birds hunted for food and recreation.

U.S. Fish and Wildlife Service: Federal agency with primary responsibility for migratory wildlife and for endangered species. Main office for South Dakota is in Pierre.

Walk-in areas: Private lands leased by the South Dakota Department of Game, Fish and Parks and posted to allow free hunting access on foot. Permission is not required but you must avoid walking in standing crops and you need to stay at least 660 feet away from livestock and occupied farmsteads.

Waste grain: Seeds from various crops such as corn, wheat, soybeans, sunflowers or other domestic plants left on the ground or on remaining plant stalks after crop harvest. These waste seeds provide high energy food sources for pheasants, grouse, and several other wildlife species.

Waterfowl: Normally used to refer to ducks, geese and swans.

Waterfowl Production Area (WPA): Land purchased and owned by the U.S. Fish and Wildlife Service and managed primarily for waterfowl but also of value to pheasants and other wildlife. These federal lands are open to the public for legal hunting. Funding for purchase of such land is primarily thorough funds raised through sale of the Waterfowl Hunting and Conservation Stamp.

West River: All land west of the Missouri River in South Dakota.

Wildlife Restoration Act or Pittman-Robertson Act (1937): More correctly, named the Federal Aid in Wildlife Restoration Act. Provides for a federal tax on arms and ammunition with funds divided up among states on the basis of hunting licenses sold and numbers of hunters. To use these funds hunting license fees for individual states must be used for wildlife management purposes and cannot be rerouted for use on highways or other non wildlife type projects. Funds from this act are known as P-R Funds or Wildlife Restoration Funds.

About the author

Les Flake is Distinguished Professor Emeritus in the Department of Natural Resource Management, South Dakota State University (SDSU), Brookings, where he primarily taught ornithology, wildlife management, and waterfowl ecology until retirement in August 2003. He has authored or coauthored numerous papers in professional research journals along with four books. He received an M.S. in Biology from Brigham Young University in 1966 and, in 1971, a Ph.D. in Zoology from Washington State University. Since retirement, Les has been living in Springville, Utah with his wife Marcia. He has returned to South Dakota each fall for two to three weeks of upland bird hunting, visiting with friends, and work with co-authors on a series of three wildlife books and a technical report for the South Dakota Department of Game, Fish and Parks (SDGFP). Les is an avid upland game bird enthusiast and long-time gun dog owner and has hunted South Dakota for over 41 years.

The author with Brook on a Game Production Area near the Missouri River in fall 2013.

Additional related photos

Hunting near the Missouri River with my first gun dog, Pepsi, in the mid 1970s. She is retrieving a sharp-tailed grouse.

Our family in Brookings in 1978. Front: Kim (left), Margo (right). Back:, left to right, the author, Ryan, and Marcia.

Over the years in South Dakota, we had three litters of Brittanies and one hybrid litter. Margo (1975) holds a pup from our first and only litter from Pepsi.

Kim with Pepsi and pups in 1975.

My son Ryan with his grandfather, Ruel Allen and our second Brittany, Rascal (about 1988).

Rascal's resume as a
pup included being a terrific pointer on upland birds, chewing
up the land-line phone on the wall, and tearing up the linoleum
on our stair landing (mid 1980s).

Kali at 7 weeks (fall 1994), a good age to bring a pup home to
meet the family.

My third Brittany Kali died at around 9 years of age of an undiagnosed illness just before I retired from South Dakota State (summer 2003). So many great points on birds and such a lonely feeling to lose her.

Gary Peterson is a long-time friend and hunting and fishing companion and is frequently mentioned in the book. He looks a bit concerned about this Alaskan brown bear.

Connie Gates at home (the "Brittany Palace") in Brookings in fall 2013 with her dog Starr (left) and my dog Brook. Connie is mentioned in Chapters 3 and 60.

When visiting Brookings I try to catch my friend and colleague Ken Higgins for a breakfast visit (November 2012). Ken has a great sense of humor (Chapters 58 and 78).

The author with pheasants and sharptails in fall 2011. Landscapes with about 70% grassland and 30% cropland can make for good populations of both pheasants and prairie grouse.

Two golden oldies. Marcia and Les vacationing in Olympia Washington in September 2014.

MAP

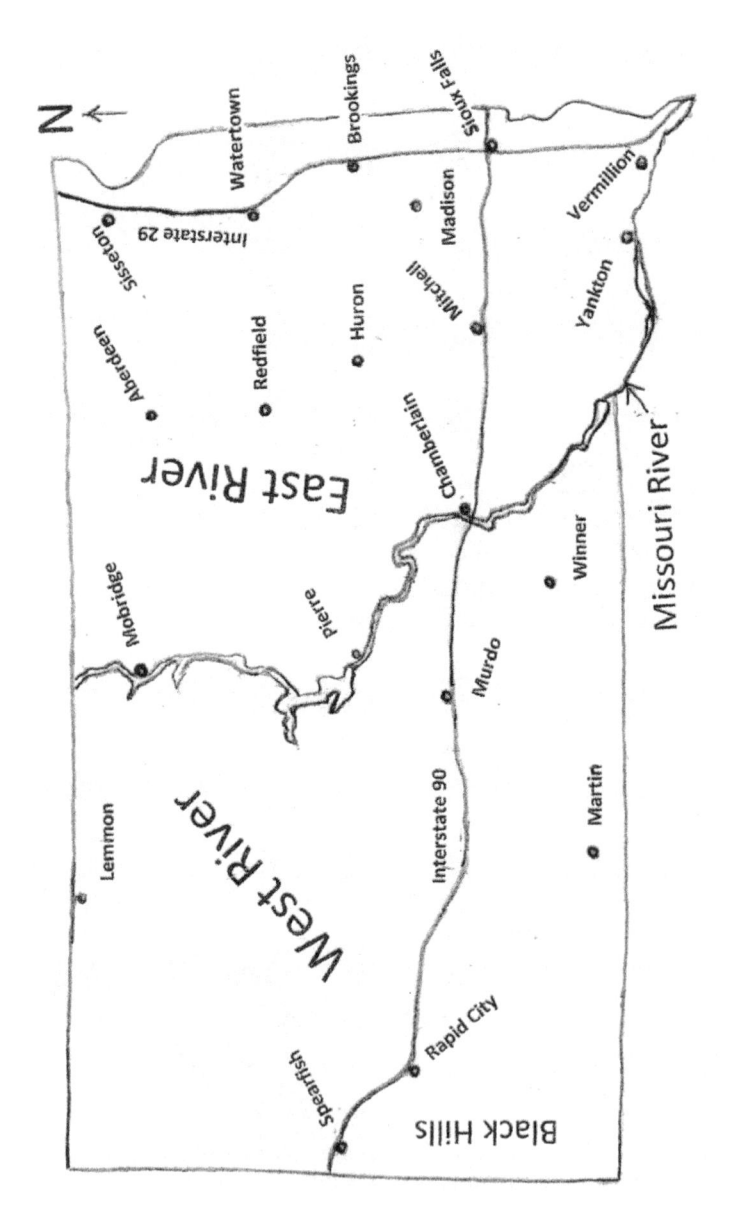

South Dakota
(about 360 miles from east to west border)

Made in the USA
Coppell, TX
30 November 2021